STANDING FIRM

STANDING FIRM

The Doctrinal Commitments of Moody Bible Institute

GENERAL EDITORS

John A. Jelinek and Bryan O'Neal

MOODY PUBLISHERS
CHICAGO

Edited by Kevin P. Emmert
Cover and interior design: Erik M. Peterson
Cover photo of Bible by Aaron Burden on Unsplash

ISBN: 978-0-8024-1910-1

We hope you enjoy this book from Moody Publishers. Our goal is to provide high-quality, thought-provoking books and products that connect truth to your real needs and challenges. For more information on other books and products written and produced from a biblical perspective, go to www.moodypublishers.com or write to:

Moody Publishers
820 N. LaSalle Boulevard
Chicago, IL 60610

13 5 7 9 10 8 6 4 2

Printed in the United States of America

*To the past, present, and future students and faculty of the Moody Bible Institute with the prayer that they will always **speak** and **live out** the things that are appropriate for sound doctrine in fulfilling their calling in Christ (Titus 2:1).*

CONTENTS

CONTRIBUTORS

Jonathan Armstrong Associate Professor of Bible and Theology; Director of the Center for Global Theological Education. BA, Cornerstone University; MA, Trinity Evangelical Divinity School; MPhil, Fordham University; PhD, Fordham University.

John K. Goodrich Associate Professor of Bible. BA, Moody Bible Institute; MDiv, Talbot School of Theology; ThM, Talbot School of Theology; PhD, University of Durham, U.K.

John A. Jelinek Professor of Theology. BRE, William Tyndale College; ThM, Dallas Theological Seminary; ThD Grace Theological Seminary.

Marcus Peter Johnson Professor of Theology. BA, Moody Bible Institute; MA, Trinity Evangelical Divinity School; PhD, Trinity College, University of Toronto.

Michael McDuffee Professor of Theology, History. BA, University of New Hampshire; MA, Wheaton Graduate School; MA, PhD, Brandeis University.

Sanjay Merchant Associate Professor of Theology. BS, University of Southern California; MA, Biola University; MA, MA, Talbot School of Theology; PhD, Claremont Graduate University.

Laurie Norris Associate Professor of Pastoral Studies. BA, Cedarville University; ThM, Dallas Theological Seminary; PhD, Wheaton College.

Bryan O'Neal Professor of Theology. BA, Moody Bible Institute; MA, PhD, Purdue University.

Gerald W. Peterman Professor of Bible. BDesign, University of Florida; MA, MDiv, Trinity Evangelical Divinity School; PhD, King's College, London.

Gregg Quiggle D. L. Moody Professor of Theology; Dean of Study Abroad Programs. BA, Wheaton College; MA, Wheaton College Graduate School; MA, Marquette University; PhD, Open University.

Steven H. Sanchez Professor of Bible; Chair of Bible and Theology Division. BA, Columbia University in the City of New York, NY; Certificate of Continuing Education, Emmaus Bible College; ThM, PhD, Dallas Theological Seminary.

Andrew J. Schmutzer Professor of Bible. BA, Moody Bible Institute; ThM, Dallas Theological Seminary; PhD, Trinity International University.

J. Brian Tucker Professor of New Testament. BS, Lee College; MA, Liberty University; MDiv, Michigan Theological Seminary; DMin, Michigan Theological Seminary; PhD, University of Wales, Lampeter.

Benjamin Wilson Assistant Professor of Bible. BA, University of Oklahoma; ThM, MDiv, Talbot School of Theology; PhD, University of Cambridge.

The Context of the
MBI Doctrinal Statement

THE SIGNIFICANCE OF THE MBI DOCTRINAL STATEMENT

Bryan O'Neal

"God bless the School that D. L. Moody founded; /
Firm may she stand, by foes of truth surrounded! /
Riches of grace bestowed may she never squander, /
Keeping true to God and man her record over
yonder."[1]

These words of the Moody Bible Institute school song serve
to bind together generations of students, alumni, faculty,
and staff, as well as express a sincere prayer that God would
continue to bless, guide, and protect the school that Dwight
Lyman Moody founded in 1886. "Standing firm" is fundamentally a matter of remaining true to doctrine and mission, a
prayer faithfully answered now for over 130 years.

Our name—Moody Bible Institute—expresses three core
components of who we have been, who we are, and who we will
be. "Moody" refers to our founder, the great nineteenth-century
evangelist, who desired to live a life fully devoted to the service
of the gospel and sought to see others equipped to participate

in the work of Christian ministry. "Institute" is an outdated word in some quarters (but not at places like the United States Military Institute or the Massachusetts Institute of Technology); it rightly reflects that we are not a liberal arts college or university, but instead are committed to producing graduates with practical skills to serve the church, whether in vocational or nonvocational roles. And, most importantly, "Bible is our middle name." The Bible is the heart of the curriculum at Moody and the core of our associated ministries in broadcasting and publishing. Without apology or qualification, we hold the Bible in the highest regard possible as inspired, inerrant, and authoritative. For us, standing firm means persevering in our mission to teach the Scriptures and to equip students, readers, and listeners to "accurately [handle] the word of truth" (2 Tim. 2:15).

Every person or organization chooses to present itself to the world in a certain way—we might think about this as the way people develop the "About" section of a social media profile. For a religious organization like Moody Bible Institute, the most important feature of our self-identity and self-presentation is our doctrinal statement. In *Standing Firm* we present afresh the doctrinal identity of Moody Bible Institute.

When walking into a mall or amusement park, most people immediately look for the map that shows the overall layout, and, most importantly, an arrow that reads "You Are Here." From a doctrinal perspective, this book serves as Moody's map and the arrow. As we say to our new students when we begin our introductory theology course, "We are Christian, we are Protestant, we are dispensational."

To call ourselves "Christian" recognizes the historic and invisible unity of the church across space and time, which in its broadest categories includes the Eastern church associated with the various strands of Orthodoxy (Greek Orthodoxy, Russian

Orthodoxy, etc.), as well as the Western church identified with Roman Catholicism and Protestantism. It is worth recognizing that until the so-called "great schism" of 1054,[2] it is anachronistic to impose backwards our current categories of Orthodox, Catholic, Protestant, and so on. There was functionally a single visible church, affirming, for the most part, shared theological commitments that continue to form us today—for example, the doctrine of the Trinity and the declaration that Jesus Christ is fully God and fully man (two natures in one person).

Recently, we celebrated the 500th anniversary of the Protestant Reformation, which began as an attempt to reform the Western church—and in particular, to reclaim doctrines of the ultimate and unique authority of the Bible and of salvation by the grace of God through faith and not as a result of our own effort. As an attempt to reform the church of its day, the Reformation can hardly be called a success. But the Reformation had an astonishing effect in that it made the Scriptures widely accessible and affirmed a personalization of the Christian faith. And as an institution with "Bible as our middle name" and the equipping of Christian workers in service to the gospel as our defining mission, it should be no surprise that we stand in the Protestant tradition.

It is important to note that when we call ourselves "dispensational," this too flows out of a foundational commitment to the Scriptures. That is, dispensationalism is not first of all about end-times prophecy or God's special plans for the Jewish people. Rather, dispensationalism is a commitment to a particular hermeneutic, or way of interpreting Scripture. In overly simple terms, dispensationalism is marked by a straightforward "literalist" reading of the Bible, of course showing appropriate respect for the historical, literary, and grammatical ways the Bible was written. Such a reading then prompts conclusions about the ordering of end-time events, or God's ongoing promises to Israel.[3] By contrast, a nonliteral or "spriritualized" interpretation of the text might say, for example, that promises made to Israel were fulfilled "spiritually" in the church, and that the Messianic Kingdom is not a literal future 1000-year period, but instead a present reality with Jesus reigning in the hearts of His people.

While we are staking out a space on the map, it would be worthwhile to take up a couple more labels. Sometimes, Moody is called "fundamentalist." Are we fundamentalist? There is a difference between "cultural fundamentalism" and "theological fundamentalism," though sometimes they run together, as they have at points in the history of the Institute. Cultural fundamentalism is usually focused on lifestyle questions, which might include prohibitions against alcohol, tobacco, dancing, movie and theater attendance, makeup, women wearing slacks, and the use of musical instruments other than organs and maybe pianos in worship. At Moody, in its history and in the present, there is certainly a range of association with cultural fundamentalism. However, our doctrinal affirmations relate not to cultural fundamentalism, but rather to theological fundamentalism.

The term "The Fundamentals" historically refers to a series of essays and booklets completed in 1915 as a response to the "modernist controversy" of the late 19th century. One of the editors of these publications was R. A. Torrey, the second president of Moody Bible Institute. These fundamentals were an attempt to defend biblical doctrines that were directly under assault by the modernists, or theological liberals, of that time. Central doctrines included:

• The authority and inerrancy of the Bible, as well as a "literalist" reading of Scripture

- A literal creation of Adam and Eve, and literal fall into sin
- The virgin birth of Jesus, and other biblical miracles
- The vicarious penal atonement of Jesus on the cross
- The bodily resurrection of Jesus
- Salvation by grace through faith
- The future bodily return of Jesus

Each of these latter points flows from the first, a commitment to a straightforward reading of the inspired Scriptures. The Moody Doctrinal Statement of 1928 reveals several connections to these fundamental affirmations—as a matter of fact, every one of them is explicitly included. That is no coincidence.

MOVING FORWARD: UNDERSTANDING THE MBI DOCTRINAL STATEMENT

First in the chapters that follow, Gregg Quiggle provides an overview of the history of the doctrinal statement at Moody, beginning with its original formulation in 1928. We will also see how the Statement has been expanded (never contracted) through a series of addenda and footnotes through the intervening decades.

Sanjay Merchant explains Article I of the doctrinal statement, which articulates the central Christian doctrine of the Trinity, or the tri-unity of God. The very earliest Christian creeds affirm the oneness of God, eternally existing in three distinct, divine persons—the Father, Son, and Holy Spirit.

Article II affirms Moody's commitments to the Scriptures. Jonathan Armstrong explains the doctrines of revelation and inspiration, as well as canonicity (how the various books of the

Bible were recognized and collected). Steven Sanchez expresses the correlated commitments of the inerrancy and authority of the Bible as the Word of God to be trusted and obeyed.[4]

The center of the Christian faith is Jesus Himself, and Article III is rich with teaching about the person and work of Jesus. Gerald Peterman addresses the topic of the person of Jesus, discussing the significance of His divine and human natures.

Andrew Schmutzer takes up the material of Article IV— namely, how God has revealed Himself as Creator and Sustainer of the cosmos and everything in it, as well as how mankind has rebelled against God and fallen into sin and judgment. Also explaining Article III, Marcus Johnson explores the saving work of Christ—what Jesus has done and is doing to secure the salvation of those who trust in Him.

Jesus loves the church enough to make her His bride (see Eph. 5), and the church is the topic of the fifth and final article of the Statement. Brian Tucker describes the nature of the church as revealed in Scripture as well as how the Bible distinguishes the church from Israel. John Goodrich summarizes material from throughout the doctrinal statement to describe "future events" (the doctrine of last things, or eschatology).

Connected to these five articles is a series of eight footnotes appended in 2000. The content and significance of each of these notes is explored in the relevant chapters. These notes allowed the Institute to press more specifically into affirmations of biblical inerrancy; the special creation of Adam and Eve, and the rejection of macroevolution; the distinction between the church and Israel; and further details about future events, among other issues.

Theology is seldom done in a vacuum and is most commonly provoked by questions and challenges posed by the culture and context. The rise of the charismatic movement in the West in the latter half of the twentieth century prompted the Institute to weigh in on the nature and role of the so-called "sign gifts" of the Holy Spirit. Significantly, Moody self-describes as holding to a "nonnormative" position on these sign gifts. This intentionally occupies middle-ground between Pentecostalism (which requires the practice of certain gifts as evidence of salvation or spirituality) and "cessationism" (which denies that certain gifts are ever present in the church today). This expresses Moody's big-tent, inclusive interdenominationalism and the call for members of the Moody community not to propagate teachings that treat such gifts as "normative," or indicative of maturity or salvation. Benjamin Wilson explains this addendum and its significance.

Similarly, social changes in the United States, including (among other things) the sexual revolution and the rise of feminism, have required the Institute to distance itself from both chauvinism on the one hand (that is, the claim that there is a difference in value between men and women) and from egalitarianism on the other hand (derived from the word *equal*, the claim that men and women are not only equal in worth and dignity but also potentially in every role in the church, home, or state). Seeking to stake out an explicitly biblical position between these two extremes, Moody also includes a statement on gender roles in ministry.

As Laurie Norris explains, the Moody position denies both chauvinism and egalitarianism. Instead, Moody affirms "complementarianism" (that men and women are equal in worth and dignity but have distinct and complementary roles in church ministry). Worth noting is that the Moody position speaks only to gender roles in ministry, and in no way addresses questions about similar distinctions in the home or state.

Western culture has turned very rapidly in its views and taboos on matters of human sexuality. Whereas once there was a general if not universal public consensus that marriage was obviously a binary relationship between one man and one woman and that sexual expression was properly restricted to married couples, this consensus rapidly eroded from the late twentieth century onward (sometimes crediting the "sexual revolution," which began the '60s), with the acceptance of premarital and extramarital sex, and the affirmation and normalization of a variety of nonheterosexual identities. In order to retain our ability to establish our own community standards and parameters and to offer pastoral counsel to the church, Moody has adopted a statement on human sexuality. While biblical teaching on human sexuality is often controversial and divisive in our times, Michael McDuffee provides compassionate and pastoral counsel about the challenge and consequences of gospel faithfulness in this matter.

While we stand firm on the doctrinal inheritance that has been passed on to us, the church of every age must also be attentive to its own context and be actively prepared to give answers to fresh challenges and questions as they arise. In a closing chapter, John Jelinek considers what affirmations the church and the Institute might helpfully provide in years to come.

While in general Moody has a long history of welcoming a "broad orthodoxy," it is clear that, in at least some of the points introduced above, Moody has also chosen to affirm some positions that are more specific and detailed. Despite these narrower affirmations, Moody continues to open as large a front door as possible to serve the church, which is to say to serve a variety of local churches and denominations through our ministries of publishing, broadcasting, conferences, and education. While these positions serve to identify our faculty, staff, and board, there are many within the Moody family, including many alumni and current students, who stand in theological and denominational streams much broader than those delineated by certain aspects of our doctrinal statement.

And we are very grateful that this is true. Indeed, the preamble to the doctrinal statement actively celebrates the variety of expression in the universal church: "While Moody's particular definitions are important to its position, it is readily recognized that they do not define orthodoxy for the whole body of Christ. Moody gladly embraces all who faithfully adhere to the essentials of biblical Christianity as fellow believers and colleagues in Christ's cause." And so, while affirming the historical doctrines of the Trinity and resurrection of Jesus are necessary markers of orthodox Christianity, we are happy to extend humble charity to those who hold other positions on things like spiritual gifts and gender roles, to use only two examples, and to celebrate their fruitful co-labor in the gospel through the ages and around the world.

It is our hope that this publication will serve as an encouragement and resource to the universal church and a fresh expression of our ongoing, faithful stewardship of the boundless riches of grace that God has bestowed upon this place and this people for over 130 years. In a culture filled with foes of truth of every sort, by the prayers of the saints and the grace of God, Moody Bible Institute continues to stand firm. May it be so until Jesus comes in glory.

THE HISTORY OF THE MBI DOCTRINAL STATEMENT

Gregg Quiggle

THE DOCTRINE OF OUR FOUNDER

Any attempt to describe the theological history of Moody Bible Institute must look back to our namesake, Dwight Lyman Moody. Moody was an evangelist, and his theological commitments were reflected in his evangelistic work. As his son William pointed out, Moody "preferred to devote his energies to evangelistic work, yielding to the denominational churches the function of indoctrinating the Christian faith."[1] Consequently, Mr. Moody is a very difficult figure to categorize theologically. He was not given to credalism, denominationalism, or theological speculation; rather, he sought to concentrate on practical religion.[2]

This does not mean Moody had no theological commitments. It does mean Moody's theological commitments reflected his calling as an evangelist. As early as the 1870s, Moody described the role doctrine played for him in evangelism. He preached several sermons explaining his concept of faith. Specifically, Moody argued saving faith consisted of three parts: knowledge, intellectual assent, and trust. Moody referred to trust as "laying hold."[4] In fact, Moody was adamant that sincerity in faith was not sufficient to save. Faith must be grounded in true doctrine. He made this very clear at Northfield in 1899:

People have an idea now that it makes very little difference what a man believes if he is only sincere, if he is only
honest in his creed. I have had that question put to me
many a time: "Mr. Moody, you don't think it makes any
difference what a man believes if he is only sincere?" I
believe that is one of the greatest lies that ever came out
of the pit of hell. Why they virtually say you can believe a
lie just as well as you can believe the truth, if only you are
earnest, you know and stick to it.[5]

Doctrine mattered to Mr. Moody.

Consequently, if you look closely at the life and work of
Moody, a basic theological framework emerges. This framework consists of six elements. First, Moody emphasized the
love of God. This was a core belief that became, to a degree, a
defining doctrine for Moody. Second, Moody was aggressively
devoted to a nonsectarian, interdenominational approach to
Christianity. This was part of his strategy to promote evangelism among all Christian churches and individuals. It also
reflected his concept of love. Third, he demonstrated a deep
commitment to the Bible and read it literally. While Moody
did not have a highly developed and nuanced doctrine of the
Bible, he clearly revered it and sought to make it normative
in his life and work. This quote sums it up nicely: "I have one
rule about books. I do not read any book, unless it will help
me understand the Book."[6] Fourth, he held to what can best
be described as the basic tenets that typified evangelical revivalists. Specifically, Moody's basic construct was the "Three Rs":
Ruined by sin, Redeemed by Christ, and Regenerated by the
Holy Ghost. These three represent the core of Mr. Moody's
gospel presentation. The final two doctrines, the Holy Spirit's

role in Christian service and premillennialism, served to distinguish him from earlier generations of revivalists.

THE EARLY DOCTRINAL COMMITMENTS OF MBI: AN INTERDENOMINATIONAL FOCUS

After Mr. Moody's death in 1899, his beliefs served as the template for the doctrinal commitments of the Moody Bible Institute. The Institute mirrored Mr. Moody in its emphasis on evangelism. In fact, from its founding in 1886 to 1899, it was called the "Chicago Evangelistic Society."[7] Its stated purpose was for the "education and training of Christian workers, including teachers, ministers, missionaries, and musicians who may completely and effectively proclaim the gospel of Jesus Christ."[8]

Again reflecting Mr. Moody, the school's doctrine during these years was nondenominational—or better, interdenominational. Like Mr. Moody, the Institute avoided publicly affirming many denominational distinctives, not because those distinctives are unimportant, but because the school's focus was to educate and train evangelistically oriented students who could serve in many denominations and ministries.

Perhaps the strongest indication of the interdenominational nature of the Institute is the fact that the school did not adopt a formal doctrinal statement until 1928. However, that did not mean the school had no theological commitments. The Bible was the core of the curriculum. It was taught extensively and interpreted literally. In fact, the academic catalogue from 1893–1894 states the primary text of all classes is the English Bible. As one reads through the mission statements and stated objectives of the Institute, the influence of Mr. Moody's commitment to the three "R"s is still evident. These three doctrines that drove Mr. Moody's evangelistic fervor and evangelism guided the Institute in its early days.

THE MBI DOCTRINAL STANCE IN THE CONTEXT OF THE FUNDAMENTALIST/MODERNIST CONTROVERSY

As the Institute moved into the twentieth century, it found itself serving Protestant churches wracked with theological turmoil. A number of denominations and schools were ripped apart. Churches divided along theological lines into what were known as Fundamentalists and Modernists, or Liberals. The Institute began formally aligning with the Fundamentalists.

The formation of Fundamentalism provided the context for the Institute's 1928 doctrinal statement. One pivotal moment for the Fundamentalists was the publication of *The Fundamentals.*[9] *The Fundamentals: A Testimony to Truth* was a set of ninety essays published between 1910 and 1915 designed to refute liberalism. The second president of the Institute, R. A. Torrey, was one of the editors. James M. Gray, the third president, was a contributor.

Another defining moment for Fundamentalists was J. Gresham Machen's lecture entitled "Christianity or Liberalism," delivered November 3, 1921, before the Ruling Elders Association of Chester Presbytery and published a year later in the *Princeton Theological Review*. In that address, Machen makes the central point that undergirding Christianity is its connection to history. As he puts it, "From the beginning, the Christian gospel, as indeed the name 'gospel' or 'good news' implies, consisted in an account of something that had happened. And from the beginning, the meaning of the happening was set forth; and when the meaning of the happening was set forth then there was Christian doctrine. 'Christ died'—that is history; 'Christ died for our sins'—that is doctrine. Without these two elements, joined in an absolutely indissoluble union, there is no Christianity."[10] Moody has always linked history and theology in our reading of the biblical text.

A third moment was the Scopes Monkey Trial of 1925. This trial was over the teaching of evolution in public schools in Tennessee. The trial was broadcast live on WGN radio in Chicago. It was the first time a trial was broadcast, and virtually every major newspaper released daily reports. From one perspective, it could be viewed as a public hearing on the validity of the Bible. With this context in place, let us turn to the development of the Institute's 1928 statement.

THE PATH TO THE MBI DOCTRINAL STATEMENT

The earliest semblance of a doctrinal statement is from 1914. It appears to be both an official and unofficial statement. The Board of Trustees minutes from December 1912 indicate a desire to pursue forming a doctrinal statement. However, in July of 1914, the Board of Trustees determined it was "unnecessary and undesirable" for the Institute to have its own statement at that time. They noted that a statement adopted as a "Conference Testimony" at the International Conference on the Prophetic Scriptures had appeared in some Moody literature. The Board indicated that they saw the statement as representing our "convictions and has our endorsement."[11]

In addition to the 1914 statement, it appears the statement developed for the World Council on Christian Fundamentals held in Philadelphia in 1919 was also formative for the development of Moody's 1928 statement. This 1919 statement became the basis for the World's Christian Fundamentals Association. The Institute published the statement in their

January 1920 edition of *The Christian Workers Magazine*.[12] On examination, the parallels with the Institute's 1928 statement are obvious.[13]

The 1928 statement was adopted with what appears to be little fanfare. The trustees' minutes record virtually no discussion surrounding the adoption of our statement. One of the most interesting things about the 1928 statement is how short it is. Given the turmoil of the times, the deliberate brevity is telling. It most likely reflected the Institute's commitment to be a nonsectarian, interdenominational school. Both Mr. Moody and the Institute as a whole tried to function in a way that respected denominational commitments—and the Institute still does to this day. The Institute tried to make simple, clear statements of basic Protestant orthodoxy that could be embraced by as many denominations as possible. Indeed, the catalog contains the following statement: "It is readily recognized that they (Moody's 1928 statement) do not define orthodoxy for the whole body of Christ. Moody gladly embraces all who faithfully adhere to the essentials of biblical Christianity as fellow believers and colleagues in Christ's cause."[14]

The statement does, however, include distinctives, just as Mr. Moody had distinctives. Mr. Moody's were premillennialism and a unique understanding of the work of the Holy Spirit. In the case of the Institute's 1928 statement, the distinctives were premillennialism and pretribulationalism. Although these two doctrines are not named as such, their implication was understood. This turn is interesting. It is clear that Mr. Moody taught premillennialism, and it was certainly the dominant position at the school before the 1928 statement. However, as late as 1923, the chairman of the board was publicly stating that premillennialism was not a precondition to speak at chapel or teach on the faculty. The emphasis on premillennialism probably reflects the impact of the previously mentioned 1926 World's Christian Fundamentalist statement.

The main body of the 1928 MBI statement remained essentially unchanged until 2017. Specifically, the statement regarding the doctrine of the Trinity was clarified. The 1928 statement was changed from "God is a Person who has revealed Himself as a Trinity in unity, Father, Son, and Holy Spirit—three Persons and yet but one God," to "God is triune, one Being eternally existing in three co-equal Persons: Father, Son, and Holy Spirit; these divine Persons, together possessing the same eternal perfections." The 1928 statement can be read to say God is a person and God is three persons. The change states more clearly God's unity and the three distinct persons of the Trinity.

Before this modification, several footnotes were added in May 2000 to clarify the 1928 statement during the Stowell presidency. These were the result of a cooperative effort between the Board of Trustees, the administration, and the faculty. The purpose of the footnotes was twofold. First, to show how the 1928 statement could be expressed relative to current concerns. Second, to explain each clarifying position using current language. For example, in Article II, a footnote affirming inerrancy was added in response to challenges raised during the "Battle for the Bible" in the '70s and '80s. Another footnote was added to affirm an explicitly dispensational hermeneutic, the distinction between Israel and the church, and an expectation of a pretribulational rapture.

Although not part of the doctrinal statement, other positions with which Moody has historically been identified have been officially supplemented. These are positions the trustees, education administrators, and faculty are expected to hold. Some are simply statements of the classic Christian position. Others are areas in which the Institute recognizes that we serve and minister with others whose traditions differ on some of these questions. The areas addressed include sign gifts, gender roles in ministry, human sexuality, and inerrancy.

In 1983, addenda clarifying the Institute's position on sign gifts were attached. The statement in part reads, "Moody maintains that there is one baptism of the Holy Spirit that occurs at the time a person is born again, placing that one into the body of Christ. Moody also distinguishes between spiritual gifts distributed to believers to equip them for ministry and the 'sign gifts,' stating sign gifts are . . . not normative for the church today." It concludes, "While this institutional position is not and must not be a test of fellowship with those whose traditions differ, members of this community will not practice or propagate practices at variance with Moody's position."[15]

In 2000, a statement clarifying general roles in ministry affirmed the dignity and worth of all believers and the priesthood of all believers. It concludes, "Moody distinguishes between ministry function and church office. While upholding the necessity of mutual respect and affirmation as those subject to the Word of God, Moody understands that the biblical office of elder/pastor in the early church was gender specific. Therefore, it maintains that it is consistent with that understanding of Scripture that those church offices should be limited to the male gender."[16]

In the 2013–2014 academic year, faculty endorsed a statement on "Human Sexuality." Initially entitled "Homosexuality and Transgenderism," the statement points out the Institute's commitment to the classic Christian position as it is presented in Scripture. The 2018–2019 Undergraduate Catalogue states,

> The first two chapters of Genesis constitute the paradigm and prerequisite for God's creative intent for human

personhood, gender and sexual identity, and sexual intimacy in marriage (Genesis 1:27; 2:24; cf. Matthew 19:4–5).

We affirm that humanity came from the hand of God with only two sexual distinctions, male and female, both bearing the image of God, and emerging from one flesh with the unique physical capacity to reunite as one flesh in complementarity within a marriage. God's creation design and intent for marriage as expressed in Genesis 2 is therefore exclusively between one man and one woman. Within this monogamous context, intended to be life-long, sexual intimacy is a glorious blessing from God.

Based on biblical theology (cf. Leviticus 18; 1 Corinthians 5–6; and other passages), we conclude that non marital sex, homosexual sex, same-sex romantic relationships, and transgender expressions are deviations from God's standard, misrepresenting the nature of God Himself. As such, these are wrong under any circumstances in God's eyes. We affirm the worth and relevance of human gender and sexuality as a distinctive of marriage. Consequently, we consider all other forms of sexual expression sinful, misaligned with God's purposes.

We affirm God's love and concern for all of humanity, a concern that compelled Him to offer His Son a ransom for our lives, and we consider His biblically recorded and specifically defined guidelines for sexual practice to be enduring expressions of His love and protection of our human identity (Matthew 19:5–9).

Our expectation is that each member of Moody's community will honor the biblical obligation to surrender
one's body to God. Non marital sexual intimacy, homosexual sexual intimacy and same-sex romantic relationships, and gender identification that is incongruent with
one's birth sex are all violations of biblical teaching from
which Moody derives its community standards. We willingly submit ourselves to these biblical mandates in light
of our call to holiness and to self-surrender.[17]

For well over a century, the Moody Bible Institute has
charted a course that places it firmly in the center of conservative, evangelical Protestantism with an eye to serving as many
churches as possible. It has committed itself to encouraging
evangelism, teaching the Bible, and providing practical ministry training through all its activities. Should the Lord tarry,
we look forward to another century of serving the church by
helping equip men and women to proclaim the good news of
the Lord Jesus Christ.

Expositions of the MBI Doctrinal Statement

ON THE TRIUNE GOD

Sanjay Merchant

God is triune, one Being eternally existing in three
co-equal Persons: Father, Son, and Holy Spirit; these
divine Persons, together possessing the same eternal
perfections, work inseparably and harmoniously in
creating, sustaining, and redeeming the world.
—ARTICLE I

Some consider the doctrine of the Trinity to be an impenetrable paradox, resulting from ancient theological nitpicking, a technical addendum to our shared faith with little practical significance for the Christian life. On the contrary, the Trinity is the central mystery of Christianity, disclosing edifying truths about God's nature and revealing the deep logic of the gospel.

Although the term *Trinity* is not explicitly recorded in the Bible, Scripture contains three relevant teachings about God's nature: (1) there is one God; (2) the Father, Son, and Holy Spirit are equally divine; and (3) the Father, Son, and Holy Spirit are distinct divine persons. Those who accept the authority of Scripture cannot believe in more than one God; or that the Son and Spirit are lesser beings than the Father;

or that the Father, Son, and Spirit are parts or personalities of a solitary divine person. The Father, Son, and Spirit are distinct divine persons who enjoy genuine communion with one another while individually and equally being the one true God. This profound idea is essential to Christian worship and proclamation.

Admittedly, we cannot describe God with scientific precision since human philosophical tools are too crude to entirely settle questions about His being. The transcendent Source of reality is beyond our comprehension. For us, "His greatness is unsearchable" (Ps. 145:3). Humans cannot pretend to completely fathom our Creator. After all, as He announced through Isaiah, "My thoughts are not your thoughts, nor are your ways My ways. . . . For as the heavens are higher than the earth, so are My ways higher than your ways and My thoughts than your thoughts" (Isa. 55:8–9). Nonetheless, early theologians developed partial analogies to help us envision God's nature and think more exalted thoughts about Him who, ultimately, surpasses our limited understanding. Meditating on divine tri-unity is both an intellectual activity and an expression of reverence as we strive to know and love the glorious God who first loved us. "Oh, the depth of the riches both of the wisdom and knowledge of God! How unsearchable are His judgments and unfathomable His ways" (Rom. 11:33). Our worship begins as we consider God's unrivaled majesty. "Before Me there was no God formed," the Lord declares. "And there will be none after Me. I, even I, am the Lord, and there is no savior besides Me" (Isa. 43:10–11). Indeed, "the Lord is our God, the Lord is one" (Deut. 6:4; see also James 2:19), who is "God in heaven above and on the earth below; there is no other" (Deut. 4:39). For this reason, the Israelites were forbidden to venerate other supposed gods and were charged to respect the Lord alone (see Ex. 20:3–4; 2 Kings 17:34–41; 1 Cor. 8:4–6).

Philosophy also indicates that there is only one maximally great being. Let us imagine, for the sake of argument, that Perfect Bob has all of God's characteristics—including infinite power, knowledge, and goodness—and ask, "Can Perfect Bob keep a secret from God?" On one hand, it seems that he cannot since God knows everything. Yet, on the other hand, Perfect Bob can prevent others from knowing his secret since he is all-powerful. The absurd answer is that God would both know and not know Perfect Bob's secret! Absurd situations, however, cannot occur, meaning that Perfect Bob cannot exist. As it turns out, there cannot be more than one maximally great being. "I am God, and there is no other; I am God, and there is no one like Me" (Isa. 46:9).

God, therefore, has no rival. The Holy One rightly asks, "To whom then will you liken Me that I would be his equal" (Isa. 40:25)? And yet, Jesus exercised authority over the Mosaic Law, claimed to inaugurate the kingdom of God through His preaching and miracles, professed to personally restore Israel, and forgave sins. Upon announcing that "I and the Father are one," His opponents threatened to stone Him, protesting that "You, being a man, make Yourself out to be God" (John 10:30–33; also see 5:18).

After His ascension, Jesus' followers proclaimed that the pre-incarnate Word, who "existed in the form of God" (Phil. 2:6), "became flesh, and dwelt among us" (John 1:14) as "the image of the invisible God" (Col. 1:15). They called Him "bridegroom" (Matt. 25:1–12; Mark 2:19) and "husband" (Rev. 21:2), titles by which Israel identified the Lord as a God of intimate concern (see Isa. 62:5; Hos. 2:16), and revered Him as "savior" (Luke 2:11; 1 John 4:14), a name that God refuses to share with any other (Isa. 43:11). Jesus identified Himself as "I am" (John 8:58), alluding to the sacred name "Yahweh," which the God of Israel had disclosed to Moses (Ex. 3:14).

And the Almighty God of Revelation, "the Alpha and Omega" (Rev. 1:8), revealed Himself to be Jesus (Rev. 1:17–18; 21:5–7; 22:12–20).

The early church generally refrained from identifying Jesus as "God," preferring "Lord" (1 Cor. 8:6), which conveys deity as the New Testament translation of Yahweh (Matt. 3:3; Mark 1:3; John 12:38; cf., Isa. 40:3; 53:1), so as not to imply that Jesus is the Father. Accordingly, Paul explained that while others worship "so-called gods . . . for us there is but one God, the Father, from whom are all things and we exist for Him; and one Lord, Jesus Christ, by whom are all things, and we exist through Him" (1 Cor. 8:5–6), thereby equating God the Father and the Lord Jesus in Christian worship. John, nevertheless, risked confusion by referring to the Word who became flesh as "God" (John 1:1) and "the true God and eternal life" (1 John 5:20). In addition, he recorded that Thomas had called the risen Jesus "my Lord and my God" (John 20:28). Similarly, Peter and Paul described Jesus as "God and Savior" (2 Peter 1:1; Titus 2:13). And the writer of Hebrews quoted Psalm 45:6 (Heb. 1:8) and 102:25 (Heb. 1:10) in referring to the Son as "God" and "Lord," respectively.

In addition to proclaiming His divine titles, the early church recognized Jesus as the Creator and Sustainer of the world (John 1:3, 10–11; 1 Cor. 8:6; Col. 1:16–17; Heb. 1:3; cf., Isa. 44:24), Pardoner (Luke 5:21; Col. 3:13; cf., Ps. 130:4; Jer. 31:34), Redeemer (Gal. 3:13; Titus 2:13–14; Rev. 5:9; cf., Ps. 130:7; Hos. 13:14), and Judge (Matt. 25:31–46; John 5:22; 2 Cor. 5:10; 2 Tim. 4:1; cf., Joel 3:12). Most significantly, Christians profess to receive God's grace and redemption *in Christ*, who is the first fruits (1 Cor. 15:20–23) and "author and finisher" of our faith (Heb. 12:2 NKJV), who wields divine power to save as the "one mediator . . . between God and men" (1 Tim. 2:5), and in whom we become new creatures (2 Cor. 5:17). He is the principal administrator of divine rescue and reconciliation, giving Himself as the substance of redemption. He does not simply offer salvation, He *is* our salvation. God, as triune, both redeems and reveals, compassionately restoring creation and disclosing Himself as the agent of restoration. The God who creates is the God who rescues; He is a Savior responding to His creation's groaning.

Of course, Jesus Christ is predominately identified as God's beloved Son (Matt. 3:17) who alone enjoys intimate knowledge of the Father (Matt. 11:27). "The Father loves the Son and has given all things into His hand" (John 3:35)—including the powers to give life and judge the world (John 5:21–22). Scripture thereby presents an analogy between divine and human fatherhood. Isaac, for example, was equal to his father, Abraham, in humanity, but obedient to him as a son. The Father, likewise, eternally generates the Son, Jesus Christ, who, being equally divine as "the only begotten God who is in the bosom of the Father" (John 1:18), professed to "do exactly as the Father commanded me" so that "the world may know that I love the Father" (John 14:31). Of course, Isaac is not the son of Abraham in precisely the same sense that Jesus Christ is the Son of God. Even if Isaac were the "spitting image" of his father, resembling Abraham far more than his mother, Sarah, he did not wholly represent Abraham in appearance and personality. But Jesus is "the exact representation of His [Father's] nature" (Heb. 1:3). Unlike human parents who contribute only part of themselves to their offspring, the impartible Father contributes His whole being to His Son. For this reason, Paul declared that "in Him all the fullness of Deity dwells in bodily form" (Col. 2:9), and when Philip asked Jesus to show him the Father, He replied, "He who has seen Me has seen the Father. . . . Do you not believe that I am in the Father, and the Father is in Me?" (John 14:9–10). Jesus literally embodies

God. Consequently, "whoever denies the Son does not have the Father; the one who confesses the Son has the Father also" (1 John 2:23).

Scripture suggests another analogy, which effectively distinguishes divine begetting from human begetting, in identifying Jesus as "the true Light which, coming into the world, enlightens every man" (John 1:9) and "the radiance of [God's] glory" (Heb. 1:3). Just as sunlight pours out of the sun, flooding the earth with light and warmth, so the Son of God pours out of the bosom of the Father as the flawless expression of God's truth and love to the world.[1] The sun analogy avoids the implication that God created Jesus at some time in the past. The eternal Father eternally begets His eternal Son, just as an eternal sun would radiate eternal light. What is more, if there had been a time before the Son existed, God would have been potentially but not actually loving. God does not *become* love; God *is* love (1 John 4:8) by nature. He must, therefore, have an eternal beloved in His Son. In other words, there was no time at which the Father existed without His Son. Neither did the Spirit begin to come forth from the Father and Son; the procession of the Spirit is eternal (John 15:26).

The Spirit is God's only provision for power by which we are "baptized into one body" (1 Cor. 12:13; cf., John 3:5), being washed and sanctified (1 Cor. 6:11), by which we receive gifts—words of wisdom, words of knowledge, faith, healing, working of miracles, prophecy, discerning of spirits, tongues, and the interpretation of tongues (1 Cor. 12:8–10)—and mature in godliness—"love, joy, peace, patience, kindness, goodness, faithfulness, gentleness, self-control" (Gal. 5:22–23). The Spirit, however, is much more than divine energy. In keeping with Jesus' testimony, John used masculine pronouns in reference to the neuter "Holy Spirit," contrary to the rules of Greek grammar: "But the Helper, the Holy Spirit, whom the Father will send in My name, He will teach you all things, and bring to your remembrance all that I said to you" (John 14:26; also see 14:16–17; 15:26; 16:13).

Jesus had scandalized His audience by claiming to wield God's authority, and His outrageous message and ministry carries on in the Spirit, who administered creation by hovering over the waters (Gen. 1:1), harmoniously wielding the singular divine power with the Father and Son, and who now comes in His name (John 7:39; 14:16–17; 15:26; 16:7–16; Rom. 8:9–10; Gal. 4:6). God's saving presence did not cease with Jesus' ascension but continues with the Spirit of truth, who wills (1 Cor. 12:11), fellowships (2 Cor. 13:14), testifies (Rom. 8:16), convicts, guides, speaks, glorifies, discloses (John 16:7–15), and is sinned against (Isa. 63:10; Matt. 12:31–32; cf., Acts 7:51; Eph. 4:30; 1 Thess. 5:19). In fact, Paul referred to the human body, interchangeably, as "the temple of God" and "the temple of the Holy Spirit" (1 Cor. 3:16; 6:19–20) and declared that "the Lord is the Spirit" (2 Cor. 3:17–18). Peter as well equated lying to the Spirit with lying to God (Acts 5:3–4). Once again, the God who loves and sends is the God who descends and redeems.

The revelation of God's divine Son exposes a personal distinction within deity. Fathers and their sons are related *individuals*. By the same token, the Father, Son, and Spirit are individuals; not the single-same divine person pretending to be three as God is neither narcissistic nor deceptive. When the Father loves the Son, He loves another. When Jesus prays to His Father, He addresses another. When the Spirit testifies of the Son, He testifies of another. But the revelation that God superintends the world through His Spirit indicates an essential unity among the divine persons. The distinct Father, Son, and Spirit share the one divine nature and, therefore, a single instantiation of eternality, all-powerfulness, all-knowingness, and perfect goodness. There are not three instantiations of each divine characteristic because there cannot be more than one God.

Early theologians—including Gregory of Nyssa and Gregory Nazianzen—proposed another analogy to illustrate that the Father, Son, and Spirit share the same being as distinct persons. Imagine a pool of liquid gold from which three identical statues emerge, as the liquid flows through them.[2] We would not ask, how many golds exist? There is just one pool of gold. Likewise, we do not ask, how many gods exist? There is just one divine being. The Father, Son, and Spirit flow into one another, sharing divinity, as the statues share the pool of liquid gold.

The sun/radiance and gold analogies capture crucial aspects about God's nature, although analogies cannot entirely convey the mystery of the Trinity. The exalted triune God ultimately exceeds our comprehension. Worshipers, all the same, adore Him who responds to creation's groaning. Salvation is reconciliation with God the Father, achieved through the atoning work of God the Son, and affected by the ministry of God the Spirit. "There is one body and one *Spirit*, just as also you were called in one hope of your calling; one *Lord*, one faith, one baptism, one *God and Father* of all who is over all and through all and in all" (Eph. 4:4–6, emphasis added). Trinitarian theology is, in large measure, an expression of the Christian experience of redemption, as evidenced by the invocation of the threefold "name of the Father and the Son and the Holy Spirit" at baptism (Matt. 28:18–19). The Trinity is integral to the apostolic message of salvation. So Paul bids the Corinthians, "The grace of the Lord Jesus Christ, and the love of God, and the fellowship of the Holy Spirit, be with you all" (2 Cor. 13:14).

The disciples touched the Son, who appeared in human flesh to atone for our sins on the cross, and witnessed the

Spirit, who descended as a dove and tongues of fire to draw us to repentance. The advent of Jesus ("Yahweh's salvation"), our Emmanuel ("God with us"), is initiated by the Father and facilitated by the Spirit. The incarnate Savior speaks at the direction of the Father (John 12:49) and works by the power of the Spirit (Luke 4:14; Acts 10:38). Christ is not one who merely demonstrates a procedure for purging personal sins through humility. The incarnation, ministry, death, and resurrection of God the Son attests that no earthly power can provide spiritual healing. God saves by giving Himself for us and filling us with His presence, spanning the chasm between heaven and earth in the persons of the Son and Spirit: His own commissioned Word and Breath, coming forth into the world.

ON THE REVELATION OF GOD

Jonathan Armstrong

The Bible, including both the Old and the New
Testaments, is a divine revelation, the original
autographs of which were verbally inspired by the
Holy Spirit.
—ARTICLE II

When we affirm that the Bible is a divine revelation, we
are saying that the Bible reveals or discloses the mind
of God. The stories that we read in the Bible—the story of the
shepherd boy who defeats a giant with nothing but a sling, or
the story of the tax collector who abandons his possessions in
order to follow Jesus along the shores of the Sea of Galilee—
are not merely surprising and time-honored tales. The Bible
communicates to us the very thoughts of God. This unique
collection of sixty-six books—written in Hebrew, Aramaic,
and Greek, across the ancient world from Babylon all the way
to Rome, and over a time span of nearly 1,500 years—reveals
God's perspectives on the creation of the world, the sinfulness
of humanity, the provision of the Savior, Jesus Christ, and
the salvation to which we look forward in the life to come.
The fact that the Bible is a divine revelation means that this

one-of-a-kind and sometimes difficult-to-understand book communicates to us the most important message that anyone could ever hope to read. At first, the proposition that the Scripture is a revelation from God might seem straightforward enough. After all, this belief has been maintained through the entire history of Christianity, and even before among the Jewish community. The ancient bishops of the Roman church believed that Scripture is a revelation, and the saints and scholars of the medieval period believed this; the great Reformers staked their lives on this truth, and the revivalists and hymn writers of the past several centuries preached and celebrated this truth. And yet, implicit in the view that the Bible is a revelation of God is a philosophical problem that can seem almost insurmountable when we begin to tease it out. How can communication between a divine mind and a human mind even be possible? How can God, who is eternal and infinitely wise, express His omniscient mind in common words? How can words give expression to the intelligence that stands behind the universe?

But Scripture is adamant that it reports to us a message from God. We cannot read even a few pages of Scripture without bumping up against the idea that there is a God and that He is a God who enters into the affairs of the world and communicates with humankind. That there is a God and that He is a God who reveals Himself is not a conclusion for which the Bible argues but rather a presupposition that is borne out by the entirety of the contents of the Bible. Reflect for a moment on the opening of the Bible, which posits simply and unapologetically: "In the beginning, God created the heavens and the earth. . . . Then God said, 'Let there be light'" (Gen. 1:1, 3). God speaks creation into existence. In this sense, all of the created order reflects God's word. Theologians, therefore, sometimes refer to this window into God's nature and purposes through the created order as "general revelation," reserving the phrase "special revelation" for God's communication specifically in the Scriptures. For the purposes of this chapter, we will reflect on "special revelation" or the way that God speaks to us in the Bible.

GOD REVEALS HIMSELF IN SCRIPTURE

Let's get back to the notion that the Bible presupposes the existence of God and that the God whom the Bible presupposes to exist is a God who reveals Himself to humankind. Why doesn't the Bible undertake to prove formally that the fact of God's existence or His nature as one who reveals Himself? Of course, one can only speculate, but it seems that if God were to prove His existence and nature as a God who reveals Himself to us by an argument that we simply could not deny, we would be no closer to entering into the sort of loving, reconciled relationship with God that He desires to foster. By way of analogy, human fathers take it upon themselves to prove their fatherhood to their children only in exceptional circumstances. It is not that the question of fatherhood is uninteresting or irrelevant—quite the contrary! But the concept of fatherhood when reduced to a technicality has almost nothing in common with the fuller sense of fatherhood that sets our expectations and hopes for our relationships. If God were to set out an infallible proof for His own existence and that the Bible is His revelation—an argument that were literally impossible to deny or to pretend were not true—He would not be the kind of God whom you would wish to exist. If God were to set out an argument proving that He is a God who reveals Himself and there were simply no possibility of escaping this conclusion, He would not be the kind of God whom you would wish to know. Put another way, if God made the fact of the revelatory quality of the Scriptures completely undeniable, it would be as though He were shouting at us so loudly that we could never learn to listen to what He is saying. The purpose of God's revelation is that we should place our confidence in Him as our Redeemer and Lord, not that we should mindlessly cede formal agreement. We should be suspect of any truth claim that is entirely self-authenticating. In our pluralistic age, there are a whole host of spiritual movements and theosophies that are ready to persuade us that they speak for a divine voice and that their revelations are not to be questioned. Fortunately for us, this is not how the God of the Bible reveals Himself.

The Bible is chock full of references to God revealing Himself. God speaks to humanity in the covenants, in His prophets, and finally in His Son, Jesus Christ, and this pattern of divine communication to humanity represents the thematic arc of the whole Bible. God speaks frequently and directly to many figures in the Old Testament. God speaks with Moses so openly that we read, "Thus the LORD used to speak to Moses face to face, just as a man speaks to his friend" (Ex. 33:11). God speaks to Abraham concerning His covenant with the son of promise (Gen. 17:21), to Rebecca concerning the birth of Jacob and Esau (Gen. 25:23), and to Jacob concerning resettling in Egypt (Gen. 46:3). Interestingly, God does not reveal Himself to Joseph—the principle character in the final section of Genesis—in direct speech but indirectly, through dreams and circumstances. However, as the narrator of Genesis tells us, God was with Joseph (Gen. 39:2), quietly orchestrating events. At the close of the book of Genesis, Joseph can see God's work in his life and declares that God had allowed the hardships of his life in order to bring about the salvation of Egypt (Gen. 50:20). Even in the texts where God does not directly speak, God is revealing Himself and His redemptive plans. Perhaps the clearest example of this is the book of Esther, wherein the word *God* does not appear in the entire book, and yet the purposes of God are impossible to miss in this story of the Jewish girl who becomes queen of Persia and saves her people. The apostle Paul writes: "For whatever was written in earlier times was written for our instruction" (Rom. 15:4; see also 1 Cor. 10:11). Paul writes at the conclusion of his life that all Scripture is inspired by God: "All Scripture is inspired by God and profitable for teaching, for reproof, for correction, for training in righteousness" (2 Tim. 3:16). As we learn from the apostle Peter, "all Scripture" is not limited to the Old Testament but includes Paul's own epistles in the New Testament (2 Peter 3:16).

There is a phrase of particular power that appears in Scripture and affirms God's nature as a God who reveals Himself, and that is "Thus says the Lord." The phrase occurs over four hundred times across the pages of the Old Testament. We read this phrase for the first time in Scripture when the Lord commands Moses to confront Pharaoh and appeal for the release of the children of Israel (Ex. 4:22). Moses and Aaron return to Pharaoh with the message: "Thus says the LORD, the God of Israel, 'Let My people go'" (Ex. 5:1). The phrase is part of the prophetic tradition and appears when God validates His own unparalleled power and authority. The phrase resounds with the forcefulness that we would expect of God when He claims His rightful place: "Thus says the LORD, the King of Israel and his Redeemer, the LORD of hosts: 'I am the first and I am the last; besides me there is no god'" (Isa. 44:6 ESV; see also 43:16; 45:18). This tradition is especially rich in the prophetic literature, wherein the prophets confront idolatry. As often as the phrase "Thus says the Lord" occurs in Scripture, it has an enduringly arresting quality.

In the New Testament, we do not encounter the phrase "Thus says the Lord," because therein we encounter Jesus Christ, the very Word of God who "became flesh and dwelt among us" (John 1:14). The author of Hebrews explains this transition: "Long ago, at many times and in many ways, God spoke to our fathers by the prophets, but in these last days he has spoken to us by his Son" (Heb. 1:1–2a ESV). Jesus is introduced to us in the New Testament as the Messiah, the fulfillment of the prophetic hope. The apostles record the words of Jesus in the Gospels and expound His teaching in the epistles. The power of prophetic tradition of the word of God from the Old Testament is applied to the Gospels. After citing the famous verse from Isaiah, "The grass withers, the flower fades, but the word of our God will stand forever" (Isa. 40:8 ESV), the apostle Peter can write, "And this word is the good news that was preached to you" (1 Peter 1:25 ESV). The good news, preached by the apostles across the Roman Empire and written down in the four gospels in our New Testament, is the same, eternal word of God preached beforehand by the prophets of God! Paul states this principle clearly when he writes to the church at Thessalonica: "When you received the word of God, which you heard from us, you accepted it not as the word of men but as what it really is, the word of God" (1 Thess. 2:13 ESV; see also 2 Thess. 2:15). Peter teaches us that prophecy does not stem from a human impulse, "but men spoke from God as they were carried along by the Holy Spirit" (2 Peter 1:21 ESV). The image in Peter's language is that of a ship being driven along by the wind. God brought about the revelation of Scripture not mechanistically but by the mystery of the Holy Spirit's prevailing presence over the prophetic and apostolic authors.

SCRIPTURE IS THE REVELATION OF GOD

Perhaps you are thinking to yourself, *It seems clear that God speaks or reveals Himself in the Bible, but surely there is a critical difference between believing that God reveals Himself in the Bible and believing that the Bible is a divine revelation.* That is true. By affirming that the Bible, including both the Old and New Testaments, is a divine revelation, we are affirming that we ascribe this quality of revelation not to any arrangement of ancient or classical literature, but specifically to the canon of texts handed down to us as the Bible. This means that we embrace every part of the Bible as revelation of God, even the parts that seem at odds with dominant political or philosophical views. The canon as a theological principle means precisely this: everything that is included in the Old and New Testaments is properly part of the Bible. The history of the canon of the Old and New Testaments—that is, where the books of the Bible circulated in antiquity, what records we have concerning which books were read in which areas of the world and at which times, and how these books were copied in the era before the printing press—is a genuinely complicated narrative and requires attention to many details in order to set out an accurate picture. But the canon as a theological principle means that we maintain that every part of the Bible, no more and no less, is revelation from God.

Christians in the tradition of Moody Bible Institute have had a century-long debate with certain biblical critics concerning whether all of the Bible—every word of every verse—is to be heralded as divine revelation. Why is it important that every word of every verse be defended as revelation and not dismissed as an "interpolation" or later addition? Why does it matter whether we receive the canonical form of the Scriptures or an amended version produced by certain biblical critics? The answer to this question is that we hold the Bible to be not merely *a* revelation from God but *the* revelation from God. What I mean is this. Suppose I handed you a letter and said, "This letter claims to be from your mother; please verify whether this is true." Presumably you would be able to tell by the handwriting and by the words and tone of the letter whether it were genuinely from your mother. However, if I handed you a letter and said, "This letter claims to be from your mother, but we believe that bits of the letter have been added by (an)other author(s); please verify whether your mother is (among) the original author(s) and which parts were certainly not written by your mother." This raises the complexity of the task vastly, but a clever critic could perhaps assemble some clues pointing toward a particular conclusion. This is how some imagine the task of biblical criticism.

To continue our illustration, let's suppose that I hand you a letter from your mother, but you have never met or knowingly spoken to your mother. In this case, you would not be in a position to judge whether a secondary author had added lines to the letter because the letter would serve as an introduction to the character of your mother. It is in this sense that we believe that the Bible serves to introduce to us the character of God. We cannot pick and choose which passages of Scripture we admit as revelation and which we dismiss as "interpolations" and still hope to arrive on an undistorted view of the nature and purposes of God. The whole story of the Bible tells us that when we listen to the voice of the tempter, who continues to ask today, "Indeed, has God said" (Gen. 3:1), we end up worshiping the idols we make in our own image rather than the God in whose image we are made.

The Bible presents itself to us as a revelation of God, and the context of this revelation is that it is addressed not to those who are confident of their relationship with God but to those who are estranged from God. We were strangers (Eph. 2:12), and even enemies of God (Rom. 5:10), but God reconciled us to Himself and made us "a chosen race, a royal priesthood, a holy nation" (1 Peter 2:9). Part and parcel of the conviction that the Scriptures are divine revelation is the understanding that the Bible communicates to us not any message but a message of reconciliation from God. God in His plan of salvation has made a way for us to be restored and made new. In this light, we should read the Bible not as a textbook but as an offer of reconciliation. And when we read the Scriptures as an invitation to reconciliation with God through the atoning work of Jesus Christ, we will never be disappointed (cf. Isa. 28:16; Rom. 10:11).

ON THE AUTHORITY
OF SCRIPTURE

Steven H. Sanchez

The Bible, including both the Old and the New
Testaments, is a divine revelation, the original
autographs of which were verbally inspired by the
Holy Spirit.[1]
—ARTICLE II

---

1. The Bible is without error in all it affirms in the original autographs and is
the only authoritative guide for faith and practice and as such must not be
supplanted by any other fields of human learning.

The conviction that the Bible has authority is a consequence of three truths. First, the Bible is a revelation from
the God who created everything we see and cannot see (Col.
1:16, Heb. 11:3). This revelation was received, understood,
and written down by those to whom it was revealed. This revelation has God Himself as its source. The second truth is that
God's character protected His original communication. A perfect God cannot communicate an imperfect revelation. Even
if He must accommodate Himself to communicate with imperfect beings, such condescension does not debase His revelation. Third, although we do not have the original autographs

in our possession, we can, with great certainty, reconstruct the original revelation.

These three facts—that God is the author of Scripture, that God's character protects His communication, and that we can reconstruct the original revelation—give the Bible ultimate authority. If we remove one of these supports, the authority of God's Word collapses, just as a three-legged stool cannot stand if you remove one of its legs.

A REVELATION FROM A GOD WHO SPEAKS

The Bible is one way God has chosen to interact with the world He created. From the beginning, He revealed Himself to be a speaking God. He is not a shy deity worried about dominating a conversation. Instead, the God of the Bible reveals Himself in actions and in words. Over and again, we read in the pages of the Bible, "God said" (appearing 52 times), "The Lord said" (274 times), and "Thus says the Lord" (over 400 times).

In contrast to general revelation, God's verbal interactions with creation are a special revelation. They are special because they reveal the mind of God in a way that wordless revelation cannot. It is one thing to witness an event that leads us to believe God is just. It is a completely different thing to hear God say of Himself,

> "For I, the LORD, love justice,
>   I hate robbery in the burnt offering;
> And I will faithfully give them their recompense
>   And make an everlasting covenant with them." (Isa. 61:8)

In the course of time, the second person of the Trinity became a human being, Jesus Christ, who lived with people and taught them using words. The writer of Hebrews acknowledged that Jesus' teaching ministry was part of a long line of messages from God when he wrote, "Long ago, at many times and in many ways, God spoke to our fathers by the prophets, but in these last days he has spoken to us by his Son" (Heb. 1:1–2 ESV). The God who spoke in times past did not abandon this method of revelation but chose to incarnate it. Jesus was greater than the prophets. They revealed what God told them, but Jesus was God incarnate speaking directly to His creation (Mark 4:39–41). The early church understood this and preserved the record of Jesus' life and teaching in the four gospels.

Some would suggest that the Bible finds its source in the creative imaginations of the religious communities that revered it. The consequence of this explanation would be that the Bible might have authority, but this would depend on whether you accept the testimony of the faith community. Someone who is not a member of that group might be inclined to reject their testimony and, therefore, reject the authority of the Bible. But the Bible gives us a different explanation.

The apostle Paul argues in his second letter to Timothy that "all Scripture is God-breathed and is useful for teaching, rebuking, correcting and training in righteousness, so that the servant of God may be thoroughly equipped for every good work." The ESV, along with the NET and NIV, translates the original Greek very literally: "God-breathed." Other versions, such as NASB and NKJV, translate it "inspired" or "by inspiration." In both cases, they indicate Paul understood that the words of Scripture have their origin in God's mind; He is their source. Therefore, they are profitable for all the uses required to make a person equipped to do good.

It is from this verse that students of the Bible derive the term "inspiration." The term does not mean that the words of the Bible are *inspiring*, but that God is their source. What is more, inspiration applies to the very words used in the Bible, and it encompasses every word in the Bible. The Moody Bible Institute, therefore, teaches the verbal, plenary inspiration of the Scriptures.

Overly simplistic understandings of the inspiration process that suggest a dictation-like approach are unfit to explain how God ensured that the words He wanted to reveal were communicated: there is mystery here! Nevertheless, answering the question of source is critical for establishing the authority of the Bible. Peter argues that prophets spoke messages that God communicated to them through the leading of the Holy Spirit. This is what gave them their authority. Without this, the words of Israel's prophets would be of little consequence, on par with other motivational musings. But with a divine source, these words become reliable, trustworthy, and authoritative. In contrast to the words of the false prophets and false teachers, Peter writes, "Above all, you must understand that no prophecy of Scripture came about by the prophet's own interpretation of things. For prophecy never had its origin in the human will, but prophets, though human, spoke from God as they were carried along by the Holy Spirit" (2 Peter 1:20–21 NIV).

Scripture itself shows that the revelatory event sometimes took place in a dream while the recipient was sleeping, other times through waking visions, other times through audible words, and still other times when the recipient was unaware that he was passing on a message from God! Regardless of the mode of revelation, God was the source. In a culture steeped in the prophetic word, it was important to combat the idea that the message of the prophets originated with the prophets themselves. Had this been the case, it would have legitimized the suggestion that prophecy has little authority because its source was human, not divine. It is true that the Scriptures bear the marks of the human recipient of the message, but these marks do not contaminate the message in a way that would impugn the character of its ultimate author: God is its source.

A PERFECT GOD SPEAKS PERFECTLY

It is the perfection of the source that guarantees the perfection of the communication. Since the God of the Bible speaks, it is not illogical to argue that the character of God protected the revelation that He communicated. That is to say, if He is perfect, then what He communicates will share His characteristics. It will be error-free, or to use the technical term, it will be inerrant. The argument rests on the character of God. Moses wrote, "God is not man, that he should lie, or a son of man, that he should change his mind" (Num. 23:19 ESV). The psalmist agreed when he wrote,

This God—his way is perfect;
    the word of the LORD proves true;
he is a shield for all those who take refuge in him.
(Ps. 18:30 ESV; cf. Deut. 32:4)

God's character protects His revelation from error. The trustworthiness and reliability of a communique from a god who cannot guarantee the truthfulness of his message is questionable! If God's character does not protect His message, then how can we know whether we may rely upon it? To have authority, the Scriptures must be characterized by the traits that God possesses. Since God speaks without error, the revelation that became Scripture must have been revealed without error. Why must this be so? Because the God who revealed it does not err. Therefore, we argue that the Scriptures are inerrant inasmuch as the God who revealed them does not lie or make mistakes.

This is the testimony of Scripture itself. At face value, it seems to be a circular argument: we use the Bible to defend the authority of the Bible. It would be fair to critique such an approach if it weren't for the fact that we are appealing to the ultimate source of truth in the universe—God as He has revealed Himself in the Bible. There is no higher authority to whom we can appeal, including our own authority. Those who claim that the Bible is not the Word of God assume they have sufficient knowledge to place themselves in judgement over the one who wrote it. This is a circular argument in the extreme, because they have become the ultimate source of their own authority.

RECONSTRUCTING THE ORIGINAL DOCUMENTS

The doctrinal statement of the Moody Bible Institute (1928) states that the doctrine of inspiration applies to the original autographs—that is, the documents upon which the first revelation was recorded. With this, the Chicago Statement on Biblical Inerrancy (1978) agrees when it says, "Inspiration, strictly speaking, applies only to the autographic text of Scripture" (Article X). Inasmuch as the original manuscripts are not in our possession, we are left to ask whether the copies we have are accurate copies of those original autographs. What is more, we must ask, do those copies share the same characteristics of the originals? Simply put, to the extent that a manuscript is a faithful copy of the original, it also shares the same author and, by implication, the same trait of inerrancy and, therefore, authority.

Although we do not have the originals, this does not mean we have been left adrift on a sea of doubt. We have sufficient copies such that we can, by comparing them, draw the very reasonable conclusion that the documents we have in our possession are accurate reproductions of original manuscripts that we no longer possess. The lack of the original autographs does not render the doctrine of verbal, plenary inspiration useless. The doctrine becomes more important because it reminds us that there is a reward for carefully analyzing and reconstructing the original revelation from the documents we have.

The study of textual criticism has demonstrated that the copies of both the Old and New Testament have been preserved at a level of accuracy that boggles the mind. It is true that the manuscripts in our possession are not perfect, but this does not prevent us from reconstructing the original revelation from what we have. While the arguments for the accurate preservation of the Old Testament differ from those used to support the New Testament, both lead to one conclusion: the Bible as we have it today is an accurate reproduction of what was revealed by God long ago. This is important because if, as some suggest, the Bible has become irreparably corrupted over time, then we can have little hope in our ability to reconstruct the original text, even with the careful work of text critics. In that case, the message originally breathed out by God has become something less than perfect in a way that renders its content less than completely authoritative.

SUPPORTING THE DOCTRINE

As one would expect, a revelation from a perfect God who created all things should be subject to investigation. It does no good to suggest that Scripture claims to be the words of God, but it has not proven to *be* the Word of God. Simply recommending that people "have faith" will not do, for God did not create the world to work this way. In fact, the Scriptures themselves do not require this but in multiple cases enjoin people to consider the evidence available to them so that they may exercise faith to believe revelation for which they have no evidence (Deut. 4; 1 Cor. 15; 2 Peter 1:16). This is an important distinction to make, lest we withhold confidence in the Bible while we await physical confirmation of every detail that confuses us. The Word of God is authoritative because its source is ultimate authority. The fact that Thomas needed to touch Jesus (John 20:27) did not make Jesus' prior testimony any less authoritative, just as the faith of Christians does not make the Bible any more authoritative. It does no good for us to say the Word of God has authority because we have faith that it does. The authority of God's Word depends on the character of God alone.

The Bible invites us to examine this truthfulness and prove it precisely because it is often provable. The frequent repetition of the command to remember what God has done is an invitation to consider that His past works are evidence that He tells the truth. This theme is very strong in Deuteronomy, for example, which was written to a generation of Israelites who were about to cross into the promised land (Deut. 4:10; 5:15). They needed to be reminded that they could trust God as He led them into Canaan. Moses did not simply appeal to faith. He did not rebuke any doubts they may have had. Rather, he exhorted them to remember what God had done in the past; those acts validated His promises about the future!

It is true that we do not have extrabiblical evidence for every single event described in the Bible, but to use that fact to invalidate the pursuit of *any* evidence is unnecessary. There was a time when Christians were forced to simply believe that all the events recorded in the Bible were true because the work of archaeologists and historians had yet to uncover facts that corroborated God's revelation. This is not the case anymore. What we have is extraordinary and sufficient to lead to the conclusion that when the Bible speaks, and is interpreted properly, it does so accurately.

These three arguments lead us to the conclusion that the Bible is authoritative and, therefore, when it comes to understanding the Christian faith and its practices, the Bible is the only source to which Christians *must* attend. This does not mean that we may not learn from other sources of knowledge, but rather that when other sources of knowledge speak in a manner that contradicts the Bible, we must pause and give careful thought to the problem. The fault may lie with our interpretation of the Bible. On the other hand, the conflict may only be apparent; it is not a true conflict. Finally, we may have misinterpreted the external data. In the final analysis, the Bible is the Word of God and is worthy of our trust.

ON JESUS CHRIST

Gerald W. Peterman

Jesus Christ is the image of the invisible God, which is to say, He is Himself very God; He took upon Himself our nature, being conceived by the Holy Spirit and born of the Virgin Mary.[2]

—ARTICLE III

---

2. Jesus Christ, the only begotten Son of God, is fully God and fully man possessing both deity and humanity united in one person, without division of the person or confusion of the two natures.

It is a privilege and a joy to know Jesus Christ and to confess these truths. Is such a confession important? Indeed, it is very important! Our Lord Jesus Himself asked the disciples, "Who do people say that the Son of Man is?" (Matt. 16:13). So, it is vital that we know who Jesus is. We will break this question into three parts: *Who* is being talked about, *how* did He become incarnate, and *why* does it matter?

WHO IS BEING TALKED ABOUT?

Our topic is Jesus Christ, the only begotten Son of God. The phrase "only begotten Son of God" is drawn from wording we find repeatedly in John's gospel, where Jesus is called "the Son of God" (1:34, 49; 5:25; 11:27; 20:31) or "the only begotten" (1:14, 18; 3:16, 18). Further, John narrates a segment of teaching that helps explain these phrases.

After Jesus heals a lame man on the Sabbath (John 5:1–9), Jewish leadership confronts Him, thinking His healing breaks the Sabbath (vv. 16, 18). In response, the Lord asserts that His Father is working and so He is working (v. 17). Further, He says that the Father loves the Son and shows Him all things that He does (v. 20), that both the Father and the Son give life (v. 21), and that the Father does not judge but has passed all judgment to the Son (v. 22). These are amazing claims! From these last two, we see that Jesus is divine, since judging and giving life are prerogatives of God alone (judging: Gen. 18:25; Deut. 32:35; Pss. 7:11; 58:11; 94:2; Rom. 3:6; 12:19; giving life: Gen. 2:7; Deut. 32:39; 1 Sam. 2:6; Ps. 104:29–30).

Then Jesus proclaims, "For just as the Father has life in Himself, even so He gave to the Son also to have life in Himself" (John 5:26). In this context, to have life in oneself is to have self-existence; it is having life simply because of who one is. Such self-existence is something that only God has. The Father has this self-existence and has granted for the Son to have this self-existence. This verse deserves careful thought. The Son is God (John 1:1, 18; Phil. 2:6), and there is only one God (Deut. 6:4; Isa. 45:5; 1 Cor. 8:4; 1 Tim. 2:5). Therefore, we must conclude that there was not a time when the Son was without this grant; from all eternity the Father grants self-existence to the Son. Yet the Son is not another God.

In the first few centuries of the church, scholars and theologians such as Athanasius (AD 296–373) and Hilary of Poitiers (310–368)—amongst many others—pondered these truths. They helped clarify what has come to be known as the doctrine of the Eternal Generation of the Son.[1] That is, the Son does not have a beginning; just as the Father has always existed, so He has always begotten the Son, always granted the Son self-existent life. Thus, the Father and the Son have eternally existed as two distinct persons in the one triune God. As was mentioned in the chapter on the Trinity, there is one God who is a plurality of persons. This plurality of persons is not three friends or three siblings. It is the Father, the Son, and the Holy Spirit in eternal triune relationship.

One of the glorious truths of the gospel is that you and I can become God's children by adoption (Scripture mostly uses "sons"; see Rom. 8:15; Gal. 4:5; Eph. 1:5). The Word (*Logos*, John 1:1), however, is the only one who exists eternally as a Son. He is "the only begotten Son of God."

But there is a situation that did not exist from eternity. That is, in time and space the eternal Son, the *Logos*, became and now is fully human. John says, "In the beginning was the Word, and the Word was with God, and the Word was God. . . . And the Word became flesh, and dwelt among us, and we saw His glory, glory as of the only begotten from the Father, full of grace and truth" (vv. 1, 14). So the Moody statement reads, "Jesus Christ is fully God and fully man possessing both deity and humanity united in one person." Now if nothing else, this is surely a cause for wonder, meditation, awe, and worship!

Why confess such a statement? In part, the confession is based on Philippians 2:5–8, a very important and beautiful passage. It reads:

In your relationships with one another, have the same mindset as Christ Jesus: Who, being in very nature God, did not consider equality with God something to be used to his own advantage; rather, he made himself nothing by taking the very nature of a servant, being made in human likeness. And being found in appearance as a man, he humbled himself by becoming obedient to death—even death on a cross! (NIV)

Reflecting on this passage, we mention the following: First, He was "in very nature God" (v. 6). We see from the next phrase that Paul defines "in very nature God" as having "equality with God" (cf. John 5:18). This is virtually equivalent to John 1:1. So we say Christ the Son is fully God.

Second, He made Himself nothing (v. 7). It is important to clarify what Paul says and what he does not say. Paul does not say that He made Himself nothing by giving something away, by giving something up, or by ceasing to be someone. Rather, He made Himself nothing by taking: "taking the very nature of a servant, being made in human likeness" (cf. Mark 10:45). Again, to say it negatively, when making Himself nothing, the Son of God did not cease to be God nor did He give up His deity. He did not temporarily surrender the independent exercise of His divine attributes (as if, with the Trinity, such a thing could happen). Indeed, the verse does not say He gave up something. Instead, one so glorious and powerful did the unexpected: He took on the very nature of a servant.

In this passage, Paul emphasizes what can be seen. The phrases "human likeness" and "being found in appearance as a man" (Phil. 2:7) do not imply mere appearance or any deception. It is not as if the eternal Son only looks like He might be a man. That perspective is the heresy called Docetism: Christ only "appeared" or "seemed" to be a man, to have been born, to have lived and suffered. Some denied the reality of Christ's human nature altogether, some only the reality of His human body or of His birth or death. That is a path we must not go down.

While His humanity and deity dwell together, there is no "division of the person or confusion of the two natures." Rather, there are two natures existing together in full harmony in one person. A new third nature is not created. Each nature retains all that is essential to it. Thus, we see that Jesus Christ does what only God can do. For example, He forgives sins (Mark 2:7); He knows people's thoughts (Matt. 9:4); He gives life to the dead (John 5:21); He is without sin (Heb. 4:15). Further, we can see that He is fully human: He has fatigue (John 4:6); He thirsts (John 19:28); He sleeps (Mark 4:38); and He weeps (Luke 19:41; Heb. 5:7). Here, the portion of the Moody statement that says "without division of the person or confusion of the two natures" is largely drawing on the Nicene Creed (AD 325) and Chalcedonian Definition (AD 451).

In part, the early church drafted the Nicene Creed as a clear, succinct statement of biblical truth about our Lord Jesus. The statement was needed because the third and fourth centuries saw some challenge to this historic doctrine of the church. The challenge was driven largely by Arius (AD 256–336). His followers have come to be known as Arians. Arians claimed that the Son did not exist from eternity. They claimed, instead, that He was begotten by God at a point in time, was the first creation of God, and so was a creature with a nature distinct from the Father. The church thought long and hard about this and so preserved for us the faith that has been once for all delivered to God's people (Jude 1:3).[2] The relevant part of the Creed states:

> [We believe] in one Lord Jesus Christ the Son of God begotten of the Father, the only begotten; that is, of the essence of the Father; God of God and Light of Light, true God from true God; begotten, not made, being of one substance with the Father; through whom all things came into being; the things in heaven and the things on earth.

HOW DID THIS COME ABOUT?

How does it come about that Jesus Christ is fully God and fully human? As the Moody statement says, "He took upon Himself our nature, being conceived by the Holy Spirit and born of the Virgin Mary." To begin answering this question, we go to Matthew 1:18–25, since Matthew says, "Now the birth of Jesus Christ was as follows" (v. 18). Of the many details that could be talked about, we will focus on three:

First, Jesus was not conceived in the typical way that a human is. Matthew stresses this. Mary, the mother of Jesus, was engaged to be married to Joseph. But "before they came together she was found to be with child by the Holy Spirit" (v. 18). After Joseph learns of the pregnancy, he still took Mary as his wife, but Scripture says he "kept her a virgin until she gave birth to a Son" (v. 25). Matthew's gospel is emphasizing that the Messiah has no human father to conceive Him. Similar is Luke, wherein the angel says to Mary, "The Holy Spirit will come upon you, and the power of the Most High will overshadow you; and for that reason the holy Child shall be called the Son of God" (Luke 1:35). Our Lord's conception is unique.

Second, Matthew explains that conception was from the Holy Spirit (vv. 18, 20). We should not be surprised. Often in the Old Testament, the Holy Spirit came upon someone and God worked in amazing ways. Take, for example, Othniel (Judg. 3:10), David (1 Sam. 16:13; 2 Sam. 23:2), Ezekiel (Ezek. 11:24), and Zechariah (2 Chron. 24:20). Similarly, the Spirit was present and active at creation (Gen. 1:2). Psalm 104 says that God works in the seasons, bringing harvests and feeding people and animals. Then verse 30 says, "You send forth Your Spirit, they are created; and You renew the face of the ground."

Third, this virgin conception happens as fulfillment of

Scripture; and again, we should not be surprised. Particularly in his first chapters, Matthew clarifies that the appearance of Jesus Messiah happens in fulfillment of many prophecies from the Old Testament. In this particular case, Matthew draws on Isaiah: "'Behold, the virgin shall be with child and shall bear a Son, and they shall call His name Immanuel,' which translated means, 'God with us'" (Matt. 1:23; Isa. 7:14).

While debates frequently abound over topics such as the nature of baptism or how election works, the confession of God the Son incarnate is an ancient and very important confession. The failure to confess that Jesus Christ has come in the flesh (1 John 4:2–3) is a failure to be Christian. There are current-day Arians and other aberrant groups who take the label Christian. Jehovah's Witnesses, for example, reject Trinitarian theology, asserting that Jesus the Son is a god, not God the Son with the same nature as God the Father. In contrast, the Church of Jesus Christ of Latter Day Saints (Mormons) claims that the Father and Son are two separate gods, both having bodies like humans do.

There are other Monotheisms that confess Jesus as a prophet but not God in the flesh. This is basically the Islamic view. There are those who confess Jesus as a wise teacher but not divine, claiming that belief in the divinity of Jesus is an invention of the early church. Many non-Messianic Jews hold to such views, as do some liberal theologians and liberal biblical scholars.

WHY DOES IT MATTER?

What is the significance to confessing the belief that Jesus Christ is fully God and fully man? Two very important entailments are the doctrine of the atonement (Jesus Christ died for the sin of the world) and the future hope of the Lord's bodily return to set up His kingdom. These precious truths are discussed elsewhere in this book. Therefore, we will restrict ourselves to three other ways this truth about God in the flesh is important to us:

The first is *revelation*. God is invisible (Col. 1:15; 1 Tim. 1:17; 6:16), but Jesus the Son is the image of the invisible God. If one sees Jesus, one sees God the Father (John 14:9). The Son is the perfect revelation of the Father. As the Moody statement says, "He is Himself very God." Jesus said, "All things have been handed over to Me by My Father; and no one knows the Son except the Father; nor does anyone know the Father except the Son, and anyone to whom the Son wills to reveal Him" (Matt. 11:27). All that Jesus the Son does is perfectly in keeping with His Father's will (John 5:30; 6:38); the Son pleases His Father at all times (John 8:29). Thus, through the Son we come to know the Father.

The second is *identification*. God, in our Lord Jesus Christ, really identifies with us in our humanity. For He Himself, in the Son, has become human and has suffered our pains. As we are sometimes fatigued, so He was fatigued (John 4:6). As we are sometimes pained by rejection, by injustice, and by distrust, so He was pained as well (Matt. 17:17; Mark 3:5; 10:14; 11:17). Hebrews tells us that the Son has been tempted in all ways just as we are, yet He was without sin (4:15). Likewise, Jesus can be a merciful and sympathetic High Priest because He Himself is human and can sympathize with our weakness (Heb. 2:17; 4:15).

The third is *imitation*. As disciples of Christ, we want to live lives that are genuinely human lives and yet lives that are lived in accordance with God's Word, lived in trust toward our Heavenly Father, lived by following the Holy Spirit. Can such a life be lived? What might such a life look like? We have a perfect example in our Lord Jesus Christ. Of course, He has no sins to confess as we do. So, our lives will fall short of His. But we have an example to follow, and Scripture itself often puts forward our Lord Jesus Christ as an example worthy of imitation:

> For you have been called for this purpose, since Christ also suffered for you, leaving you an example for you to follow in His steps, who committed no sin, nor was any deceit found in His mouth; and while being reviled, He did not revile in return; while suffering, He uttered no threats, but kept entrusting Himself to Him who judges righteously; and He Himself bore our sins in His body on the cross, that we might die to sin and live to righteousness; for by His wounds you were healed. (1 Peter 2:21–24)

The eternal Son made Himself nothing and became a servant. Following His example, with His divine help and guidance, we can do the same: we can serve others, since we have already been served! Such service, in imitation of the Son, is not shameful, but glorious.

ON CREATION AND THE FALL

Andrew J. Schmutzer

Man was created in the image of God but fell into
sin, and, in that sense, is lost; this is true of all men,
and except a man be born again he cannot see the
kingdom of God; salvation is by grace through faith
in Christ who His own self bore our sins in His own
body on the tree; the retribution of the wicked and
unbelieving, and the rewards of the righteous are
everlasting, and as the reward is conscious, so is the
retribution.

—ARTICLE IV

As early as the Apostles' Creed (about AD 390), Christians
have claimed, "I believe in God the Father Almighty, creator of heaven and earth."[1] One can hardly find a more foundational and comprehensive claim of faith than attributing the
grand expanse of the universe—"heaven and earth"—to our
Creator God (see Deut. 31:28; Pss. 69:34; 96:11; Isa. 1:2).
The central text is Genesis 1–2, the great "downbeat" of design
and dignity. While many cultures, ancient and contemporary,
have their own creation stories, the biblical account is both *in*

and *against* Israel's surrounding cultures. Here are some distinguishing features of Scripture's account of creation.

CREATION

The Identity of God. God is both sovereign and personal (Gen. 1 and 2). When God reveals Himself, He reveals Himself as Creator. In fact, the primary text of creation does not speak of a God who first was, and then who acted, but of a God who makes known His nature and will in His creative action.[2] So, the doctrine of creation teaches that God is not to be equated with the universe (pantheism); because God created all things, matter and spaces are not evil (dualism and Gnosticism); nor is God organically linked to the world (panentheism). Rather, Scripture teaches that God is distinct from His world (transcendent), yet also intimately relating with it (immanent). Creation theology includes both the physical realm of objects and creatures as well as the spiritual realm of angels.

Unlike the ancient stories of Israel's world, God has no birth, nor does He have a wife, nor does God sexually engage to create. Instead, only God is divine and He created a world that functions by His laws, not a fertility scheme. Such erroneous worldviews are still present today. Scripture does not speak much about God-in-Himself or humankind-in-itself, but rather through a dynamic *relational ecosystem* that surrounds the Creator. Here, we find the "creational bindings" of God in relation to the world, humankind with God, man with woman, and humankind with the ground and animals. Ultimately, one finds Jesus as God's response to humanity's deepest need.[3]

Without Rival Deities. While polytheistic views have always been around, biblical creation knows no rival gods or negative forces that God had to fight. Genesis does, however, "put down" objects of idolatry that people worshiped in Israel's day, like the sun and the moon. Using a polemic, Scripture strips these heavenly bodies of their names, calling them merely "the greater" and "the lesser" lights (Gen. 1:16). God not only created them, but also sovereignly controls them (Gen. 1:17). Similarly, the "great creatures of the sea" (Gen. 1:21 NIV) are not monsters coeternal with God (cf. Ps. 74:13) but are mere animals that God created (Hebrew, *bara*; cf. Gen. 1:1).

Creation from Nothing. It is through speech that God reveals Himself as supreme Creator. In fact, nothing is made if God does not speak: "Let there be!" (Gen. 1:3, 6, 14, etc.). The psalmist celebrates this: "By the word of the LORD the heavens were made . . . he spoke, and it came to be" (Ps. 33:6, 9). The message of creation in the Old Testament is the unassailable power of God's words that are rooted in the authority of the Cosmic King Himself (Ps. 95:3–5). So there is no pause between God's word and its accomplishment: "and it was so."[4] God's words always take form. These themes sharpen in the New Testament, which explicitly argues that "what is seen was not made out of things which are visible" (Heb. 11:3). In the New Testament, Christ is the Mediate Creator, the focus in whom "all things hold together" (Col. 1:16–17).

Creation focuses more on *what* and *why* (concerns of function), rather than *how* and *when* (concerns of science). What fascinates biblical writers is not the metaphysical state of pre-creation, but God's creative ability to usher in what is utterly new (see Isa. 40–55).[5] Creation occurs when God asserts His sovereignty. Not surprisingly, the creation account unfolds in majestic cadence and development. Days 1–3 bring order to the "formless," while Days 4–6 fill the "empty" with inhabitants. A literary progression brings balance and symmetry to God's world: from distant (Gen. 1:2) to dearest (Gen. 1:26), inanimate to animate, and general announcement ("Let there be") to priestly blessing ("Be fruitful and multiply . . . rule," Gen. 1:28). Appropriately, creation responds: "The heavens declare the glory of God . . . day after day they pour forth speech . . . their words to the ends of the world" (Ps. 19:1, 2, 4 NIV). Creation is the beginning of God's reign as Cosmic King.

The Value of Humankind. In the panoramic account of Genesis 1, humankind is the climax of God's eight creative acts. Similarly, humans are at the center of the localized "nest" of Genesis 2. "God created humankind because God loves us and chose to reach forth, as it were, out of himself, to create things 'other' than himself, to commune with them and enjoy fellowship with them."[6] It is primarily in relation to humankind that we hold the doctrine of creation as vital. While all forms of life are made "after their kind" (Gen. 1:11, 21), only humans are made "in the image of God." This grounds identity—not in him or herself—but in God. We are image bearers who have gender, rather than genders who have image. Ours is yet another culture that has emphasized gender without an adequate foundation.

Humankind is the most unique of God's creation. Only after their creation do we hear the assessment "very good!" (Gen. 1:31). Humankind is created, blessed, provided for, given wide permissions, commissioned, but also subjected to slight restrictions (Gen. 2:16–17).[7] They certainly are not the harassed servants of ancient gods. Instead, human beings are made in God's image (Gen. 1:26). Humankind is God's under-king, charged with responsibility for the world on God's behalf. Being an image bearer is both representational and relational. Notice how the Creation Mandate to multiply and develop creation immediately follows (Gen. 1:28). This royal charge (Ps. 8:5–6) requires a physical body. This is the representational side of being an image bearer. A person does not *have* a body or an image of God, but it could be said that a person *is* a body and an image.

Sabbath Rest. This was celebration of creation completed. The seventh day was memorialized for Israel as a day of worship and service to God (Ex. 20:8). Having no "evening and morning," the Sabbath day is special, opening into the eschatological future, highlighting God's willingness to enter into ongoing fellowship with humankind.[8] Such liturgical rest was unique to Israel, stripping worship from astrological bodies. God was the Master of both *space* and *time*.

In the New Testament, Jesus declared that all who come to Him by faith would receive His rest (Matt. 11:28). As God had delivered His people out of paganism and darkness, so everyone who believes enters spiritually into the Sabbath rest (Heb. 4:8–11). For this reason, the Sabbath was not only the sign of the Sinai covenant (Ex. 31:13), but became the day of celebration for Christians on Sunday, memorializing Christ's resurrection ("Lord's day," 1 Cor. 16:2; Rev. 1:10). All who are transformed spiritually in Christ will also be transformed in body for the promised rest that awaits the return of the Lord and the creation of a new heaven and a new earth (Rev. 14:14; 21:1–4).

THE FALL

Moody also believes in the doctrine of the fall. In Christian theology, this refers to an event of when the first couple sinned in rebellion against God. The specifics of their temptation and sin are found in Genesis 3:1–8. Among other things, the fall is a catastrophic disruption of the entire relational ecosystem.[9] Judaism, however, does not view sin or the fall emerging from the early chapters of Genesis. Nevertheless, Judaism does see the escalating rebellion in the stories of Genesis 1–11, which poignantly sets the stage for the election of Abraham (and eventually the nation) as God's chosen agent.

While "the fall" is not a technical phrase found in Scripture (just as *Trinity* is not found in Scripture), Christian doctrine has derived this concept from the narrative of Genesis 2–3, and primarily from Paul's writings (see Rom. 1:18–3:23; 5:12–21; 1 Cor. 15:21–22). The theology of the fall comes from the broader teaching of Scripture, with its persistent address of sin and the need of all people for Christ's redemption.[10]

The dire results of human sin in the fall are vividly described in the Old Testament. Rebellion is evident:

"Sons I have reared and brought up,
but they have rebelled against Me. . . .
But Israel does not know,
My people do not understand." (Isa. 1:2–3)

"Hear, you deaf! And look, you blind, that you may see!" (Isa. 42:18)

Moreover, people refuse to worship their Creator:

They sin more and more,
and make for themselves molten images,
idols skillfully made from their silver . . .
They say of them, Let the men who sacrifice kiss the calves!" (Hos. 13:2)

This has a twisted result:

They exchanged their glory
for the image of an ox that eats grass.

They forgot God their Savior,
who had done great things in Egypt. (Ps. 106:20–21)

The Genesis Story. The Lord God placed the human couple in
a garden that He made both beautiful in appearance and filled
with fruit bearing trees. In fact, everything God made was
"very good" (Gen. 1:31). But two trees are uniquely described:
the tree of life and the tree of the knowledge of good and evil.
With abundant provision, the LORD God instructs Adam that
he can "freely eat" from "any" tree in the garden (Gen. 2:16).
However, Adam is commanded not to eat from the tree of the
knowledge of good and evil (Gen. 2:17). In further provision,
the LORD God forms and then brings the woman to Adam as
his indispensable companion, his mirror image.

The *fall from innocence* occurs as follows. The serpent en-
gages the woman in debative dialogue on his terms. In fact,
the serpent succeeds in raising doubts about God's goodness
(Gen. 3:1), the repercussions of disobeying God's command,
and denying the penalty of death altogether (Gen. 3:4). For
her part, the woman attempts to correct the serpent, but in
her own wording, she belittles their privileges, qualifies God's
generosity, employs vague language, expands God's prohibition, and minimizes the penalty. Simply put, these include
overstatements she cannot defend ("must not touch it," Gen.
3:2–3 NIV). She usurps God's prerogative of determining what
is "good," then she takes, eats, and gives some to Adam who is
right by her (Gen. 3:6).

Sin and Consequences. The decisions of humanity's first parents have consequences for their progeny in a propensity for
evil and the resulting moral alienation.[11] The effects of their
rebellion shatter the relational ecosystem God made. They ate,
and together they feel a naked-shame, they make temporary
clothes, and then they hide from each other and their Maker.

The "bindings" that held creation together now break apart—between humans, with animals, the ground, and God. The new reality is one of relationships torn apart.

God interrogates the three parties (Gen. 3:8–13). No party comes away free from negative consequences. Adam struggles to admit the truth and implicates "the woman" (Gen. 3:12). God then questions the woman who, in turn, implicates "the serpent" (Gen. 3:13). It is the woman who connects all three parties. So these are not isolated judgments. Having no covenant relationship with the serpent, the LORD God begins with the animal, issuing verdicts in the order of their transgression (Gen. 3:14–19): serpent, woman, and man. Each judgment has a twofold expression: (1) affecting what is central to the identity of that party (2) and also regulating an external relationship.[12]

God had promised death for disobeying His command (Gen. 2:17). Adam and Eve immediately die spiritually, but physically only later. An initial sign of their death is being prevented from eating from the tree of life. God states, "He must not be allowed to reach out his hand and take also from the tree of life and eat, and live forever" (Gen. 3:22 NIV). In other words, the fruit of the tree of life was continually eaten in order to restore human life. Prior to their sin, God did not deny them access. Adam and Eve never possessed immortality in the garden, so initially they were not denied access to the tree. Moses later develops this theme for the nation, when he challenges them, "This day I call on the heavens and earth as witnesses against you that I have set before you life and death, blessings and curses. Now choose life . . ." (Deut. 30:19–20 NIV). God's blessing fosters life, and cursing brings death. Later, Israel would also be banished from their land.

Eve craved a wisdom that was not hers to grasp (Gen. 3:6). Both she and Adam broke God's commandment (Gen. 3:17), determining what was good and evil for themselves. While Christian tradition speaks of "original sin," the word *sin* is not actually used in Genesis 3. Instead, Adam and Eve rebelled against God—their reckless pursuit of wisdom was an act of sinful hubris.[13] Following the lead of the serpent, they mistrusted their Creator who had provided lavishly for them. The serpent rejected everything that God had affirmed. God's judgment against the three parties shows that there will be ongoing hostility—the serpent will eventually lose in his conflict with the woman; the woman will live in relational antagonism with the man (her point of origin); and the man will live in ongoing antagonism with the ground (his point of origin).

Sin Is Pervasive, but Hope Is Persistent. Though still made in the image of God (cf. Gen. 9:6), humankind became dying creatures, victims of a self-inflicted wound that is theologically described as the fall.[14] Against a creation steeped in death, Paul teaches that humankind is dead in the wake of Adam, the father of humankind (1 Cor. 15:21–22). Paul certainly knew that the word *'adam* in Hebrew was both a personal name and a designation for all humanity. In his preaching to Gentiles, Paul states, "The God who made the world and all things in it, since He is Lord of heaven and earth, does not dwell in temples made with hands. . . . He Himself gives to all people life and breath and all things; and He made from one man every nation of mankind to live on all the face of the earth" (Acts 17:24–26). In effect, humankind daily endorses Adam's attitude of sin, and so shares in his liability. Everyone sins on his or her own volition.[15] Fortunately, Christ—the last Adam—has conquered death: "So also in Christ all will be made alive" (1 Cor. 15:22). It is the resurrection of Christ that guarantees our resurrection. Those who follow the "last Adam" are re-created in Christ's image. They become a new people and share in a new creation (Rom. 8:29). In Revelation, God is praised for His majestic control of His world (Rev. 10:6; 14:7; 21:1). The antiphonal chorus of the twenty-four elders sings: "You are worthy, our Lord and God, to receive glory and honor and power, for you created all things, and by your will they were created and have their being" (Rev. 4:11 NIV).

ON SALVATION

Marcus Peter Johnson

Jesus Christ is the image of the invisible God, which
is to say, He is Himself very God; He took upon
Himself our nature, being conceived by the Holy
Spirit and born of the Virgin Mary; He died upon the
cross as a substitutionary sacrifice for the sin of the
world.

—ARTICLE III

Man was created in the image of God but fell into
sin, and, in that sense, is lost; this is true of all men,
and except a man be born again he cannot see the
kingdom of God; salvation is by grace through faith
in Christ who His own self bore our sins in His own
body on the tree.

—ARTICLE IV

As a rule, doctrinal statements are not designed to say all
that can be said, and Moody Bible Institute's 1928 doctrinal statement is no exception to that rule. No ecclesial or
institutional attempt to neatly summarize the revelation of
God in Holy Scripture is able to articulate *all* that might be
faithfully said on any given doctrine revealed to us in God's
Word. When at once we recognize this, we can appreciate what
has been said and why it is important. The 1928 Doctrinal
Statement of the Moody Bible Institute (MBI) does not set out

to elaborate a comprehensive articulation of *any* biblical teaching, let alone the topic of this essay: salvation (soteriology). The biblical teaching on salvation—as I am sure the original framers of Moody's statement would be quick and glad to affirm—is so vast, deep, and rich as to escape a mere summary statement. The modest purpose of MBI's statement is to faithfully articulate several key elements of a biblical understanding of salvation—elements that are foundational for those seeking to serve Christ and His church in the ministry of the gospel, in accordance with the mission of Moody Bible Institute.

THE SUBSTITUTIONARY DEATH OF OUR SAVIOR

The first of these key elements comes from Article III of Moody's doctrinal statement, and it reads as follows: "Jesus Christ is the image of the invisible God, which is to say, He is Himself very God; He took upon Himself our nature, being conceived by the Holy Spirit and born of the Virgin Mary; He died upon the cross as a substitutionary sacrifice for the sin of the world." We do well to appreciate in this sentence Moody Bible Institute's unswerving commitment to historic, orthodox Christianity. Much of its language is drawn directly from the words of the Nicene Creed, perhaps the most important of all truly Christian confessions (doctrinal statements), a confession upon which all Christian traditions agree. Moody Bible Institute gladly affirms, with the church in all ages and all places, that Jesus Christ is God Himself in human nature. It is this joyful affirmation that undergirds any truly Christian doctrine of salvation. After all, when Christians confess that Jesus is the Savior of the world, we unanimously confess that He is that Savior precisely and only because He is both fully and unreservedly God, and fully and unreservedly human.

After all, if Jesus is not fully God, then the salvation we have in Him is not from God; and if Jesus is not fully human, then that same salvation has not reached into our humanity.

When, with gladness and delight, Christians confess together that Jesus is fully God and fully man, we are then liberated to proclaim that "Jesus died upon the cross as a substitutionary sacrifice for the sin of the world." A picture, we often say, is worth a thousand words. But so, too, is a sentence like this. For it is here, in this theologically pregnant sentence, that we enter into the nerve center of the glorious gospel: God would stop at nothing to redeem us from our sin, not even a humiliating, shameful, excruciating crucifixion. God's love for sinners is so grand and so inexhaustible that He is entirely willing, in the person of His dearly beloved and eternal Son, to die for our sin, that we may be made forever His. In the place of us sinners, who deserve the condemnation of our sin, Jesus Christ took that condemnation for us. As both fully God and fully man, He accepted, in tears and agony, the full weight of the just punishment of our sinfulness. The God-man bore our sinfulness and bore it away in a perfect and once-and-for-all sacrifice, dying for us in an act of sacrificial love that has no parallel or equal. Jesus, we are right to affirm, put sin to death, and death to death. In Jesus Christ, our sins are fully and finally forgiven, and we have everlasting peace and communion with God forever: "For it was the Father's good pleasure for all the fullness to dwell in Him, and through Him to reconcile all things to Himself, having made peace through the blood of His cross; through Him, I say, whether things on earth or things in heaven" (Col. 1:19–20).

THE RESURRECTION AND
ASCENSION OF OUR SAVIOR

The second key element of Moody's Doctrinal Statement regarding salvation comes also from Article III, which goes on to state that Jesus Christ "arose from the dead in the body in which He was crucified; He ascended into heaven in that body glorified, where He is now our interceding High Priest." Again, we are right to hear a strong echo of the Nicene Creed, where Christians together confess that "on the third day [Jesus Christ] rose again in fulfilment of the Scriptures; He ascended into heaven and is seated at the right hand of the Father." While it is most certainly true that the death of Jesus is necessary for the salvation of sinners, His resurrection is no less necessary. After all, as the apostle Paul insists, "If Christ has not been raised, then our preaching is vain, your faith also is vain" (1 Cor. 15:14). In Holy Scripture, the death of Jesus Christ is always held in an inextricable connection with His resurrection. His death is inexplicable and meaningless apart from His resurrection from that death, and His resurrection is similarly meaningless apart from His death and burial. Taken together, they constitute God's final overcoming of the death and sin that plague humanity. The staggering reality of the fact that Jesus "arose from the dead in the body in which He was crucified" is that Jesus has overcome sin and death with a resounding finality. Before the resurrection of our beloved Savior, death and sin sought to have the last word for our fallen human condition: "Death spread to all men, because all sinned" (Rom. 5:12). And yet, right in the midst of the reign of death, that last word was overcome by the Word, in the death and resurrection of the Son of God, whose new life born from a tomb was God's decisive and definitive repudiation of the reign of sin. The risen life of our Lord is the new life of humanity for all who are in

Him, freed as we are from the deadly stranglehold of sin. That is why all Christians proclaim and sing in concert with Holy Scripture, "O death, where is your victory? O death, where is your sting?" (1 Cor. 15:55). In the resurrection of Jesus Christ, death's victory has been vanquished and its sting has been stayed. For when Christ raised Himself from the dead, in the power of His Father and the Holy Spirit, He was not raised alone—He raised us with Him. He took our lowly bodies, subject as they were to the specter of death, and crucified us with Him, so that He might raise us to new and everlasting life in His glorious resurrection. "For if we have become united with Him in the likeness of His death, certainly we shall also be in the likeness of His resurrection" (Rom. 6:5).

As magnificent as it is that Jesus was crucified and resurrected for our salvation from sin and death, there is yet more to say! "He ascended into heaven in that body glorified, where He is now our interceding High Priest." This sentence from the Doctrinal Statement echoes the unfathomably good news that, having raised us with Him, Jesus now takes us to the right hand of God the Father almighty. "But God, being rich in mercy, because of His great love with which He loved us, even when we were dead in our transgressions, made us alive together with Christ (by grace you have been saved), and raised us up with Him, and seated us with Him in the heavenly places in Christ Jesus" (Eph. 2:4–6). God has made us alive in the resurrection of Christ, and has us seated with Him in the heavenly realms in such a way that Jesus is and remains our everlasting intercessor before God the Father; Jesus is our great and eternal High Priest, whose intercession on our behalf is never-ending and never-failing (Heb. 4:14–16; 7:23–25). Jesus *was* our salvation, He *is* our salvation, and He forevermore *will be* our salvation.

ONLY JESUS IS SAVIOR

The third key element of Moody Bible Institute's Doctrinal Statement regarding salvation comes from Article IV, which is stated as follows: "Man was created in the image of God but fell into sin, and, in that sense, is lost; this is true of all men, and except a man be born again he cannot see the kingdom of God; salvation is by grace through faith in Christ who in His own self bore our sins in His own body on the tree." Perhaps the most basic of all Christian confessions is that Jesus Christ is Lord and Savior. When we confess this fundamental truth, we are making a significant assumption: that we need saving! The context for any doctrine of salvation is a doctrine of sin; after all, our confession that Jesus is our Savior is unintelligible unless He saves us *from* something. Moody's statement about sin is necessarily brief but not, therefore, lacking in either truthfulness or profundity.

Humankind, simply stated, "fell into sin, and, in that sense, is lost." We should not let the brevity of the statement obscure its depth. To state that humankind fell into sin and is lost is shorthand for the expansive teaching in Holy Scripture that, as a result of the fall, humankind has become condemned, corrupted, and, indeed, alienated from God. "This is true of all men," as the doctrinal statement puts it. There are no exceptions. Not one. The fall of humanity into sin began with Adam and Eve, but it extends to every last one of their progeny; that is to say, all of humanity is in need of salvation in Christ Jesus. In obedience to God's Word, Moody Bible Institute rightly confesses that "except a man be born again he cannot see the kingdom of God." This confession comes directly from the lips of Jesus (John 3:3) and is reflected throughout His Word in the consistent assertion that new and eternal life, a life that has overcome our fall into sin and death, is available only in and through Jesus: "Blessed be the God and Father of our Lord Jesus Christ, who according to His great mercy has caused us to be born again to a living hope through the resurrection of Jesus Christ from the dead" (1 Peter 1:3). Just as all humans are necessarily born into the first Adam—and, therefore, into sin, condemnation, and death—so too, all humans require a new birth in the second Adam, Jesus Christ, in order that we may be liberated from our tragic condition and brought into the everlasting enjoyment of the blessing and kingdom of God forever.

Our entrance into the reconciliation and peace that Jesus Christ has secured between God and men is an act of pure and utter grace. That is exactly why Moody's Doctrinal Statement includes, in concert with the historic Protestant evangelicalism and in fidelity to God's Word, that "salvation is by grace through faith in Christ." Salvation, as the notes elaborating upon Moody's statement go on to specify, "is the free gift of God's grace through faith alone, in Christ alone" (endnote 3). Moody's commitment to historic Protestant evangelical orthodoxy is evident here. The Protestant Reformers labored long and hard and faithfully to restore the church to the biblical conviction that salvation can be neither purchased nor earned. The good works, virtue, and morality born out of our self-generated effort can never, and will never, avail for us before God. In short, we cannot "work" our way to salvation, however good our intentions may be: "As it is written, 'There is none righteous, not even one'" (Rom. 3:10).

It is through Christ alone, and most importantly, *in* Christ alone, that we become the recipients of God's mercy and forgiveness, found solely in Christ. And it is through faith that we receive Christ, and all that He has done for the salvation of humanity. "For by grace you have been saved through faith; and that not of yourselves, it is the gift of God; not as a result of works, so that no one may boast" (Eph. 2:8–9). The same scriptural truth is declared in Acts 13:38–39: "Therefore let it be known to you, brethren, that through Him forgiveness of sins is proclaimed to you, and through Him everyone who believes is freed from all things, from which you could not be freed through the Law of Moses." Works and boasting are excluded; indeed, all merely human achievement is excluded, because in Christ we come to know that God's mercy, love, and grace are unalloyed and unqualified—salvation is a pure and an utter gift, and that gift is Jesus: "For God so loved the world, that He gave His only begotten Son, that whoever believes in Him shall not perish, but have eternal life" (John 3:16). It is for this reason that Moody's statement reiterates and gives specificity to what it has stated in Article III ("He died upon the cross as a substitutionary sacrifice for the sin of the world"), by confessing that our faith is in Christ, "who Himself bore our sins in His own body on the tree" (1 Peter 2:24 NKJV). What Christ has accomplished for the redemption of sinners, in His death and resurrection, is something He *alone* could do.

How might we summarize Moody Bible Institute's doctrinal commitments regarding salvation? By affirming (1) that Jesus Christ, who is both fully God and fully man, died on the cross as a full and final substitutionary sacrifice for the sins of the world, effecting redemption and reconciliation between God and man; (2) that Jesus Christ rose bodily from the dead, and ascended into heaven, establishing both His comprehensive victory over sin and death, and His ongoing intercession for all those who belong to Him; (3) that the grace and mercy of God for a humanity fallen and lost in sin is found solely and alone in Jesus Christ when, through faith alone, we are born again in Him and become the recipients of His sin-bearing death and life-giving resurrection as a pure and undiluted gift.

When at once we recognize the necessary limitations and parameters of an institutional doctrinal statement, we are in a position to appreciate where Moody Bible Institute has been ready to stand for well over one hundred years. These fundamental elements that constitute Moody's statement on salvation are utterly faithful to the prophetic and apostolic testimony to Jesus Christ in God's Holy Scriptures. They are also, it is no small thing to say, entirely consistent with historic Protestant evangelicalism. Without saying it all, the doctrinal statement says what it must. By highlighting the glorious necessity of the work and person of Christ who, in death and resurrection, has become the Savior of the world, Moody's statement is worth embracing, whether in 1928 or in 2019 and beyond. To say that each and every employee of Moody Bible Institute is "required" to affirm what is stated above is to sell the truth well short. In point of fact, we all affirm what is written with great joy and conviction. We do so in grateful obedience to the calling and privilege God has given us to prepare students for ministry in service to the gospel of our Lord Jesus, and to His holy bride, the church.

ON THE CHURCH

J. Brian Tucker

The Church is an elect company of believers baptized
by the Holy Spirit into one body; its mission is to
witness concerning its Head, Jesus Christ, preaching
the gospel among all nations; it will be caught up to
meet the Lord in the air ere He appears to set up His
kingdom.

—ARTICLE V

R eflection on the nature, membership, and mission of the
church occurs rarely these days. This creates significant
confusion as to what the church is, who is part of it, and what
it should be doing. Assistance navigating out of this confusion
is found through revisiting the wisdom of those who thought
about these issues over one hundred years ago. Two doctrinal
affirmations of the Moody Bible Institute offer a center and
a circumference for the church's makeup and mission in the
world today.

Article V affirms that "the Church is an elect company of
believers baptized by the Holy Spirit into one body; its mission is to witness concerning its Head, Jesus Christ, preaching
the gospel among all nations; it will be caught up to meet the

Lord in the air ere He appears to set up His kingdom (Acts 2:41; 15:13–17; Ephesians 1:3–6; 1 Corinthians 12:12–13; Matthew 28:19–20; 1 Thessalonians 4:16–18)."[1] In 2000, Moody Bible Institute added notes that elaborated on the original Doctrinal Statement. The article on the doctrine of the church was at that time further defined. Footnote 7 clarified the earlier statement's intended definition of the church: "The Church of Jesus Christ is a distinct entity from Israel in the ongoing program of God. Further, this universal Church consists of all who possess saving faith in the death and resurrection of Jesus Christ from Pentecost to the Rapture of the Church and which will represent every language, people and nation."[2] Then, footnote 8 explained further the future biblical context relating to and the time-related considerations of the church: "Christ will return in the air preceding the seven-year Tribulation at which time He will receive into heaven all believers who constitute His church. During that tribulation period, God will bring salvation to Israel and the nations while exercising judgment on unbelievers."[3] The original Statement and the 2000 elaborations eventually became key identity markers among many fundamentalists and conservative evangelical interpreters who relied on the hermeneutical practices associated with J. N. Darby, E. F. Ströter, J. J. Brookes, A. J. Gordon (a close friend of D. L. Moody), C. E. Scofield (a follower of Moody), and the premillennial dispensational tradition. This also means that the ecclesiological point of view evident in the Statement and its elaborations reject the covenant theology perspective. The interpretive cruxes between these traditions include: (1) a distinction between Israel and the church; (2) the New Testament church as a mystery not anticipated by the Old Testament believers and thus a parenthesis in God's program; and (3) the rapture of the church preceding a seven-year tribulation period. One implication that emerged from these interpretive choices is that many within the dispensationalist tradition accused covenantal interpreters as holding to the idea that the church has replaced Israel as God's people. So, standing firm in regards to the doctrine of the church as understood by Moody Bible Institute means that an interpreter affirms: (1) the beginning of the church on the day of Pentecost; (2) Spirit baptized, that is, elect-believer membership; (3) the rapture as the ending point for the church/church age; (4) the proclamation of the gospel as its mission; and (5) the Israel and church distinction with its rejection of the idea that the church has replaced Israel as God's people.

THE BEGINNING OF THE CHURCH

Many interpreters today claim that "the church did not begin at Pentecost."[4] However, this view is not persuasive. It is more likely that the church began at Pentecost for the following reasons. First, the mystery nature of the church suggests that it is one of the aspects of the gospel that is new in contrast to much of it that has its basis in Israel's scriptural tradition (Eph. 5:32). This view highlights the agency of Paul's writings in the development of the earliest Christ-movement's beliefs concerning the church. His Damascus road revelatory experience is the point in which Paul initially recognized the connection between Christ and His "body" the church (Acts 9:1, 4; 1 Cor. 15:9). The mystery was not only revealed to Paul; it was also being revealed to others, especially as it relates to the inclusion of non-Jews as part of God's family without having to first convert to Judaism (Eph. 3:5–6; Acts 10:34–36; 15:13–17).[5] Often, in contemporary evangelical settings, the doctrine of the church is downplayed. Marcus Johnson thinks that making a close connection between the gospel and our view of the church is crucial for overcoming the contemporary crisis in ecclesiology—that is, the doctrine of the church.[6] This is particularly important because all too often, the focus is on the gospel, and the church then is seen as secondary. For Paul, the connected mystery of the gospel and the church is crucial, a connection that could only occur after the coming of Messiah Jesus.

Jesus' teaching in Matthew's gospel concerning the church is another reason to see the beginning of the church at Pentecost. Jesus says to Peter, "Upon this rock I will build My church [Gk. *ekklēsia*]; and the gates of Hades will not overpower it" (Matt. 16:18). Covenant interpreters will highlight here not a future promise to establish the church but a promise of "covenant preservation" or a "redemptive-historical preservation"— that is, the church will prevail throughout history and not be defeated.[7] The use of a Greek construction called "predictive future" in "I will build" indicates something that will come to pass or take place.[8] This does not indicate the specific timing of the beginning of the church, but Matthew 16:21 suggests it is subsequent to Jesus' death, resurrection, and ascension (see further Eph. 1:19–23). Matthew 16:18 is the first use of *ekklēsia* in the New Testament canon; it occurs in the Gospels only here and then twice in Matthew 18:17. The term has three general meanings: "a regularly summoned legislative body," "a causal gathering of people," or "people with shared belief."[9] It is often difficult to discern which nuance is being emphasized, and so decisions on this should be made based on the context; but the majority of the New Testament uses are connected to the final category: "people with shared belief." This lexical information, however, is only one aspect of this discussion. *Ekklēsia* functions differently based on theological perspectives. For example, it is likely that in Matthew 16:18, the universal church is in view, and in 18:17, a specific local group of Messiah-followers is the focus. These conclusions are based on their use in their context but also on a prior belief in the distinction between the universal and local church, a distinction not all conservative theologians would grant, but one explicitly part of Moody's Doctrinal Statement.

Ephesians 1:19–23 indicates that Jesus' death, burial, and ascension are crucial for the establishment of the church. Only after these could the church come into existence. God has "appointed" Christ "to be head over everything for the church, which is his body" (Eph. 1:22–23 NIV; cf. 1 Cor. 12:13; Col. 1:18). This is the first time *ekklēsia* is used in Ephesians, and here the term has in view the universal church, all Jews and Gentiles in Christ between Pentecost and the rapture. Jesus' death was necessary for the "Helper" to "come" (John 16:7), the church's hope rests on the resurrection (1 Cor. 15:12–19), and the promise of Spirit baptism was given in the context of the ascension (Acts 1:5). The "body" into which believers are placed in Ephesians 1:23 is the body of Christ, and this occurs only through the baptism in the Holy Spirit, which first occurred in Acts 2:1–4, 41. In Acts 11:15, Peter refers back to the day of Pentecost as "the beginning," in regard to the outpouring of the Spirit, suggesting that is when the church began. Norman Geisler connects Paul's letters and Acts by stating, "The mystery church of Paul's later epistles originated at Pentecost."[10]

SPIRIT BAPTISM

Spirit baptism is that which brings a person into the church. This is a work of the Spirit during the church age, an era that begins on the day of Pentecost and was not an experience of those in an earlier epoch. In 1 Corinthians 12:13, Paul writes

"For by one Spirit," which is a reference to the Holy Spirit's work, "we were all baptized." The "we" here refers to all those in Christ, and "baptized" refers to those who are part of the universal body of Christ. So, through the work of the Holy Spirit, all believers are incorporated "into one body." This is a good description of what the Moody Doctrinal Statement describes as the universal church: "all who possess saving faith in the death and resurrection of Jesus Christ from Pentecost to the Rapture of the Church." The "one body" here, then, is not just a reference to the local church, but to the new-covenant community between the day of Pentecost and the rapture. This membership in the "one body" does not erase existing identities. Paul continues, "Whether Jews or Greeks, whether slaves or free." The first pair is most important for the doctrine of the church that is distinctive for Moody Bible Institute, since it maintains a continuing covenantal identity for Israel, one that has not been taken over by the church. Members of the "one body" are in-Christ Jews and in-Christ non-Jews. There is no social status or situation in which a person finds themselves that will hinder them from responding to the call to be in Christ, or that is incommensurate with an in-Christ identity (1 Cor. 7:17–24).[11] Paul concludes the verse: "And we were all made to drink of one Spirit." The word *drink* here indicates that personal salvation is in view for membership within the church. Those in the one body of Christ are incorporated into Him as a result of God's prior election that is made evident in history by a person's faith response to Christ, which itself is connected to the baptizing work of the Spirit (Eph. 1:3–6). Spirit baptism of "an elect company of believers into one body" is foundational for Moody Bible Institute's Doctrinal Statement regarding the constituency of the church.

THE RAPTURE

While the beginning of the church is on the day of Pentecost, the completion of it, or at least the church age, occurs at the rapture. It is at that time that all the members of Christ's body, both alive and dead, will be "caught up together" in order "to meet the Lord in the air" (1 Thess. 4:16–17). Then, as noted by MacArthur and Mayhue, "From that point forward, the church will be in the presence of her Savior for all eternity (cf. Rev. 22:3–5)."[12]

THE CHURCH'S DISTINCT NATURE AND MISSION

The newness of the church on the day of Pentecost and the baptizing work of the Spirit of believers into the body of Christ lead to the conclusion that the church in the new covenant is distinct from Israel in the old covenant.[13] The Moody Doctrinal Statement elaborations, as mentioned above, says, "The Church of Jesus Christ is a distinct entity from Israel in the ongoing program of God." The church is not a mixed community of believers and unbelievers, as it is in covenant theology, and thus the latter sees more continuity between the church and Israel. John Frame says it this way: "Israel was the church of the old covenant; the New Testament church is the Israel of the new covenant, what Paul calls 'the Israel of God' in Galatians 6:16."[14] Frame, like many interpreters, thinks Paul has redefined Israel in such a way that its covenantal identity has been given to the church (see also Rom. 9:6). However, the referent in the Galatians verse is debatable and need not be understood to refer to the church. It is more likely that the "Israel of God" refers to historical Israel, as recipients of a blessing along with the nations.[15] Paul consistently uses "Israel" to refer to the historic nation and does not use it to refer to the church.

The "ongoing program" in footnote 7 of the elaborations along with the earlier phrase from the main Statement "to set up His kingdom" combine to clarify the idea that the church is not the kingdom, though it does relate to it in some way. For Charles Ryrie, the "Davidic" kingdom is future and relates to Israel; this is the "kingdom" in view in the Moody Statement (Acts 1:6–8). However, Ryrie also recognizes that there is a "universal" or "mystery form" of the kingdom that does implicate the church in asymmetrical ways.[16] Those who are part of the church are "people of the kingdom" (Matt. 13:38 NIV), though its full establishment awaits the future. Members of the body of Christ embody righteous patterns of life seen in Matthew 5–7 through the empowerment of the Holy Spirit. The mission of the church is to proclaim the kingdom message, or as Moody's statement describes it, "to witness concerning its Head, Jesus Christ, preaching the gospel among all nations" (Matt. 28:19–20). Michael Vlach sees the "intersection" between the gospel and the message of the kingdom in the way that "salvation qualifies one to enter God's kingdom (John 3:3)."[17] Members of the church are promised "future rewards in the kingdom for faithful service now" (2 Tim. 2:12; Rev. 2:26–27; 3:21; 5:10).[18] So while there is a distinction to be made between God's program for Israel and that for the church, there is some overlap, though the primary focus of the church is gospel proclamation and the fulfillment of the Great Commission.[19] The tension here has given rise to progressive dispensationalism, an approach within the tradition that seeks to bring to the fore a more robust understanding of the social implications of the gospel.[20] Standing firm on the doctrine of the church requires interpreters to lean back into the tradition affirmed in the Moody Doctrinal Statement while simultaneously pushing forward to embody that tradition in new and diverse contexts in order to be faithful in fulfilling the church's mission in a changing culture.

ON THE LAST THINGS

John K. Goodrich

He will come again personally and visibly to set up His Kingdom[4] and to judge the quick and the dead.
—ARTICLE III

The retribution of the wicked and unbelieving and the rewards of the righteous are everlasting, and as the reward is conscious, so is the retribution.[6]
—ARTICLE IV

It [the church] will be caught up to meet the Lord in the air ere He appears to set up His kingdom.[8]
—ARTICLE V

---

4. It is Moody's position that this refers to the premillennial return of Christ at which time He will set up His millennial reign and, at that time, fulfill His promises to Israel.
6. This statement excludes any position that asserts a temporary or complete cessation of consciousness or merging with eternal oneness or annihilation of the damned or a "second chance" or a period of suffering or purification in preparation for entrance into the presence of God.
8. Christ will return in the air, preceding the seven-year tribulation at which time He will receive into heaven all believers who constitute His church. During that tribulation period, God will bring salvation to Israel and the nations while exercising judgment on unbelievers.

It is easy to underestimate the significance of thinking rightly about matters of eschatology—the study of last things. Normally, eschatology is the last topic covered in any systematic account of theology. Yet eschatology is deceptively important. Indeed, it provides the framework for the Christian worldview, grounds our future hope, and supplies powerful motivation for sanctification and service.

Because of the significance of end-times details, Moody has taken specific stances on matters relating to individual and corporate eschatology. In this chapter, we exposit the relevant portions of Articles III, IV, and V of Moody's Doctrinal Statement by elaborating on four key points relating to the Institute's views on the last days—namely, the premillennial return of Christ, the future restoration of national Israel, the pretribulational rapture of the church, and the divine provision of eternal rewards and retribution.

THE PREMILLENNIAL RETURN OF CHRIST

Moody's eschatology begins with a commitment to premillennialism. "Pre-millennium" literally means "before one thousand years." Premillennialism, therefore, is the belief that at His return, Jesus Christ will establish an earthly kingdom that will endure for a thousand years—or perhaps simply a very long time. While most dispensational interpreters read Revelation 20 as describing a literal thousand-year reign of Christ on the earth, the precise length of this earthly reign is less important to its adherents than the mere fact of its occurrence *following* the Lord's second coming. Premillennialism is distinguishable from postmillennialism, which maintains that Christ's return will occur after His long reign. According to postmillennialism, the fundamental building blocks of the eschatological kingdom (including massive societal reform) will be set increasingly in place until it climaxes in Christ's visible installation as ruler of the world. Premillennialism is also to be distinguished from amillennialism, which posits that Jesus' return will coincide with the establishment of the eternal state, the New Jerusalem. For amillennialists, then, there will be no special earthly millennial kingdom; Christ reigns now at the right hand of the Father, and that reign will be further subjected to the Father at Jesus' second coming (1 Cor. 15:25–28), when the new heavens and new earth are installed.

To be fair, adherents of all three millennial views concur on several important fundamental points. All agree, for instance, that the Old Testament promised that sometime following the Babylonian captivity, God would establish His rule over the entire world (Isa. 2:2–4; Jer. 16:14–21; Ezek. 37:26–28), a rule to be mediated through a biological descendant of David who will reign over Israel forever (Isa. 11:1–10; Jer. 23:5–8; Ezek. 37:24–25). All agree that the New Testament unequivocally identifies this Davidic ruler as Jesus Christ (Luke 1:31–33; Rom. 1:1–4; Rev. 22:16), who spent much of His earthly ministry preaching the nearness of God's kingdom (Mark 1:14–15). Furthermore, all agree that God's kingdom has already been inaugurated and that the Davidic covenant will be consummated at Jesus' return, when He will be installed as ruler of the world (Matt. 25:31–46). What distinguishes premillennialism from amillennialism and postmillennialism, however, is the belief that Christ will return *prior to* His earthly, millennial reign and that this reign marks a phase of the eschaton (prophetic future period) distinct from the eternal state.

The notion of an eschatological earthly kingdom that follows Jesus' second coming and yet precedes the eternal state surfaces in several scriptural passages. Zechariah, for example, promises a day when Yahweh will rescue Israel from its oppressors and will establish His reign "over all the earth" (Zech. 14:9). At that time, "Jerusalem will dwell in security" (14:11), and the surviving nations "will go up from year to year to worship the King, the LORD of hosts, and to celebrate the Feast of Booths" (14:16). Importantly, sin will still exist during this period of God's reign, for the prophecy speaks of those "families of the earth" who will refuse to "go up to Jerusalem to worship the King," and so will be deprived of God's blessing (14:17). This period must precede the eternal state, for, according to the biblical record, once the new heavens and new earth have been established, suffering will cease (Isa. 65:17–19; cf. Rev. 21:4) and "all mankind will come to bow down before [Yahweh]" (Isa. 66:23).

Turning to the New Testament, the premillennial return of Christ is explicitly attested in the final chapters of Revelation. Christ's thousand-year reign is reported in Revelation 20 not only to commence upon His return to earth, once He comes for His bride (Rev. 19:7–9) and destroys His earthly enemies (19:11–21), but also to coincide with the binding of Satan (20:2), when the devil will "not deceive the nations any longer, until the thousand years [are] completed" (20:3). It must be that this millennial period is distinct from the church age, since the New Testament teaches that Satan currently remains unbound and "is now working in the sons of disobedience" (Eph. 2:2; cf. 2 Cor. 4:4). Moreover, the millennium must be a phase of Christ's reign separate from the eternal state, since the contemporaneous binding of Satan is distinguishable from the final defeat of Satan, death, and Hades (Rev. 20:7–15) and this defeat precedes the inauguration of the eternal state (Rev. 21:1–22:5).

THE RESTORATION OF NATIONAL ISRAEL

There are two main versions of premillennialism in existence today: historic premillennialism and dispensational premillennialism. Although these versions agree on the timing of Christ's return in relation to the millennial kingdom, they generally differ on two related issues—the future of national Israel and the timing of the rapture. The former will be the focus of this section, the latter the focus of the next.

Historic premillennialism normally maintains that God has no distinct eschatological plans for national Israel, because in Christ "there is neither Jew nor Greek" (Gal. 3:28), for Christ "made both groups into one" (Eph. 2:14)—namely, the church. Many historic premillennialists concede, with the majority of scholarship, that the New Testament anticipates a large-scale eschatological conversion of the Jewish people at or just prior to Jesus' return (Rom. 11:2–27). They deny, however, that Israel's role in God's eschatological program includes anything like a national or political restoration that places the Jewish people at the center of God's millennial activities. Dispensational premillennialists, on the other hand, advocate just the opposite: God's plans for Israel are irrevocable (Rom. 11:29) and thus will manifest eschatologically not only in the conversion of some totality of the Jewish people, but also in the reestablishment of the people of Israel as a geopolitical entity—over which Jesus will rule prosperously for a millennium, and through which He will bless the nations of the earth.

Evidence for Christ's future rule over national Israel is replete in the Scriptures. Indeed, it is difficult to deny that God promised throughout the Old Testament that Israel would eternally possess the land given to them. National occupation of the land was a central provision of the Abrahamic covenant (Gen. 12:1–3; 15:18–21; 17:1–8), one that Israel would enjoy from the Canaanite conquest to the Assyrian and Babylon captivities (Josh. 13:8–19:51; 2 Kings 17:14–23). Further, included in God's promises were important stipulations about reoccupation of the land following exile, promises that (at best) were partially fulfilled in the postexilic period but are awaiting complete fulfillment in a future eschatological moment (Lev. 26:4–45; Deut. 30:1–5; Isa. 11:11–16; Jer. 30:1–22; Ezek. 34:25–31; Amos 9:11–15). Taken together with the conclusions drawn above, dispensationalists believe that at or just prior to Jesus' second coming, God will regather the scattered tribes of Israel; and during the millennium, He will rule over the reconstituted nation through the mediation of His Jerusalem-based Messiah.

When we turn to the New Testament, however, there is a conspicuous paucity of explicit references to God's promises concerning the land and Israel's restoration. Many readers of the New Testament, therefore, assume that God's promises to national Israel have been either reneged or universalized, such that there is now complete parity between Jews and Gentiles with respect not only to *salvation* (Rom. 3:23–24) but also to *vocation*. But the alleged silence concerning the particularity of future Israel is more apparent than real.[1]

Luke–Acts, for example, has for many years been fertile ground for scholarly investigation into the New Testament's expectations concerning Israel's future.[2] Hope for the restoration of Jerusalem (symbolic as the capital is for *all* Israel) is implied in Jesus' message concerning the city's destruction, when He predicts that many Jews "will fall by the edge of the sword, and will be led captive into all the nations; and Jerusalem will be trampled under foot by the Gentiles *until the times of the Gentiles are fulfilled*" (Luke 21:24, emphasis added). The temporal limitation placed upon this promise (noted by the "until" clause) suggests that Jerusalem will not lay in ruins forever, for there will come a day when God will restore the city—namely, when its occupants confess the name of Jesus (Luke 13:35). Indeed, it is because of this hope that (1) Jesus promises the twelve disciples they "will sit on thrones judging the twelve tribes of Israel" (Luke 22:30), (2) the disciples ask the risen Christ about the timing of His "restoring the kingdom to Israel" (Acts 1:6), (3) Peter preaches about "the period of restoration of all things about which God spoke by the mouth of His holy prophets from ancient time" (Acts 3:21), and (4) Paul declares before the Jewish leaders in Rome how he had been imprisoned "for the sake of the hope of Israel" (Acts 28:20). In sum, the New Testament's vision concerning the particularity of Israel's future, though less consistently pronounced than in the Old Testament, is evident nonetheless.

THE PRETRIBULATIONAL RAPTURE OF THE CHURCH

A second issue about which premillennialists disagree concerns the so-called rapture. The rapture is the forthcoming, eschatological event at which Christians alive on earth "will be caught up together with [deceased believers] in the clouds to meet the Lord in the air" (1 Thess. 4:17). The phrase "caught up" is a translation of the Greek *harpazó*, which appears in the Latin Vulgate as *rapio*, from which we get the English word *rapture*. Strictly speaking, nobody ought to question whether the rapture will occur; Paul himself tells us it will in the above passage. The real question concerns when it will happen.

There are several nuanced positions concerning the rapture's timing. The two most common opinions are referred to as pretribulationalism and posttribulationalism. Posttribulationalism posits that the rapture will occur *after* the so-called great tribulation, whether the tribulation is understood to extend for the entirety of the church age, the beginning of it, or for a briefer time span (about seven years) immediately preceding Christ's second coming (see Matt. 24:42; Rev. 7:14). Regardless of their understanding of the tribulation's length, posttribulationists believe that Christians who remain alive when Jesus returns will, as Paul's discourse explains, ascend to meet Him in the clouds, even as He is descending to earth to defeat His enemies and establish His millennial reign. Yet the apparent pointlessness of this ascension is one of the difficulties premillennialists find with posttribulationalism. Why will believers be caught up to the clouds only to return immediately to the earth?

Pretribulationalists, on the other hand, regard this ascent to be with Christ as the provision of God's promised protection during the tribulation. The New Testament consistently describes the days immediately preceding Christ's return as involving unprecedented suffering. God, however, pledged to safeguard His people from this dark time: "Because you have kept the word of My perseverance, I also will keep you from the hour of testing, that hour which is about to come upon the whole world, to test those who dwell on the earth" (Rev. 3:10; cf. Jer. 30:7; 1 Thess. 1:10; Rev. 7:13–14). Indeed, returning to gather His followers to a heavenly abode is precisely what Jesus promised to His disciples: "If I go and prepare a place for you, I will come again and receive you to Myself, that where I am, there you may be also" (John 14:3). If, then, this premillennial gathering coincides with the catching up of believers in 1 Thessalonians 4:17, then the rapture's timing fits best before, rather than after, the seven-year tribulation.

ETERNAL REWARDS AND RETRIBUTION

Perhaps the most contested eschatological issue in the church today concerns the afterlife, particularly the question of final destinies. Paul maintains that "each one of us will give an account of himself to God" (Rom. 14:12). But what are the possible outcomes of this accounting? Who will receive rewards and who will receive retribution? Competing views abound in our contemporary world, many of which are not well tethered to the plain sense of Scripture. Yet against the mounting pressure of religious pluralism, Moody maintains that eternal rewards will be issued exclusively to believers in Jesus Christ, while unbelievers will receive eternal punishment.

The Bible promises various eschatological rewards for followers of Jesus—most notably, eternal life. This will be issued in distinct phases. In the first place, God will grant believers postmortem disembodied life in heaven where they will reside with God (Phil. 1:23–24). This is what theologians normally refer to as the intermediate state. However, the Christian's final phase of existence will involve physical resurrection and the receipt of imperishable bodies (1 Cor. 15:35–49; 2 Cor. 5:1–2). Beyond everlasting life, Christians will be awarded places of relative prominence in the millennial and eternal kingdoms. God is not a cosmic Marxist; rewards will be issued in accordance with one's earthly sanctification and service.[3] As Jesus explained, those who have been "faithful with a few things" will be placed "in charge of many things" (Matt. 25:21, 23; cf. Luke 19:17, 19).

In parallel fashion, God will judge those who fail to embrace the gospel by consigning them to hell. Contrary to those who teach that God's retribution will be temporary (purgatory) or unconscious (annihilationism), Moody maintains the traditional, literal view of hell, whereby unbelievers will be separated from God and experience eternal, conscious punishment.

The unceasing nature of God's retributive justice is suggested at key moments throughout the biblical witness. The prophets speak repeatedly of those who have transgressed against Yahweh—how "their worm will not die and their fire will not be quenched" (Isa. 66:24). Jesus likewise teaches how unbelievers "will go away into eternal punishment" (Matt. 25:46). The consciousness of hell, moreover, is suggested when Jesus repeatedly likens the experience of this punishment to "weeping and gnashing of teeth" (Matt. 8:12; 13:42, 50; 22:13; 24:51; 25:30). While the image of gnashing teeth probably conveys anger, the notion of weeping indicates suffering, and together they imply consciousness.[4] Paul similarly attests that the Lord Jesus will issue "retribution to those who do not know God and to those who do not obey the gospel of our Lord Jesus. These will pay the penalty of eternal destruction, away from the presence of the Lord and from the glory of His power" (2 Thess. 1:8–9).

Moody's eschatology is accurately summed up by the label *dispensational premillennialism*. Everything stated above is standard fare for those who adopt that designation. Yet it has not been our goal in this essay to demonstrate that the Bible is perfectly clear on all matters of eschatology—because it isn't. We will invariably have greater confidence about the grander points of theology than the finer ones, and some aspects of eschatology are quite fine indeed. Still, it is Moody's conviction that Scripture sufficiently attests to the doctrinal commitments defended here, and the Moody community proudly embraces those who stand with us.

Doctrinal Positions
of the
Moody Bible Institute

ON THE SIGN GIFTS OF THE HOLY SPIRIT

Benjamin Wilson

Moody maintains that there is one baptism of the Holy Spirit that occurs at the time a person is born again, placing that one into the body of Christ. Moody also distinguishes between spiritual gifts distributed to believers to equip them for ministry and the "sign gifts" which are understood to have been manifestations of the Holy Spirit to authenticate the messenger and the gospel message during the foundational period of the church. Therefore, Moody holds that "sign gifts" are not normative for the church today. While this institutional position is not and must not be a test of fellowship with those whose traditions differ, members of this community will not practice or propagate practices at variance with Moody's position.

The work of the Holy Spirit is one of the most precious privileges experienced by the body of Christ. As believers living after the outpouring of the Holy Spirit at Pentecost, we experience God's ongoing presence and empowerment in a way that saints of prior stages in salvation history could only look forward to longingly. The Spirit's presence and work are central to our daily Christian experience, and there is quite a bit of diversity in how different Christian traditions have conceived of this crucial aspect of the Christian life. Therefore, Moody's doctrinal statement includes an addendum on the spiritual gifts to spell out how we understand and seek to experience the presence and empowerment of the Holy Spirit.

THE PRESENCE OF THE HOLY SPIRIT

There are two key doctrinal positions that are presented in our statement about the spiritual gifts. First, Moody's statement takes a position regarding the nature of the presence of the Holy Spirit in the life of the believer. The Statement reads, "Moody maintains that there is one baptism of the Holy Spirit that occurs at the time a person is born again, placing that one into the body of Christ."

When a person believes in Christ, that person is radically made new by the regenerative work of the Holy Spirit. They are "born again" and placed into a new family of brothers and sisters in the Lord. And all believers, all members of the body of Christ, receive the full measure of the Holy Spirit at the moment of their conversion.

Thus, in Romans 8:9, Paul makes it clear that belonging to Christ and possessing the Holy Spirit go hand in hand. The verse states, "However, you are not in the flesh but in the Spirit, if indeed the Spirit of God dwells in you. But if anyone does not have the Spirit of Christ, he does not belong to Him." In other words, there are no members of the body of Christ that do not possess the Spirit. If a person genuinely belongs to

Christ, then that person possesses the full measure of the Spirit of Christ.

Similarly, in Acts 2:38, at the end of Peter's sermon at Pentecost, Peter assures his audience that if they repent and are baptized into the name of Jesus Christ for the forgiveness of sins, they will receive the gift of the Holy Spirit. Regardless of their age or ethnicity or knowledge of the Scriptures or lifestyle prior to their belief in Christ or any other factor in their personal backgrounds, all those in Peter's audience who believed in Christ were promised the gift of the Spirit. It is a gift that is common to all believers. Hence, Paul in 1 Corinthians 12:13 can state, "For by one Spirit we were all baptized into one body, whether Jews or Greeks, whether slaves or free, and we were all made to drink of one Spirit." All those in Christ share in the same Holy Spirit without exception.

This understanding of the Holy Spirit's presence is distinct from some Pentecostal traditions that encourage believers to seek a second baptism of the Holy Spirit to propel them toward greater intimacy with God and new gifting in His service. In such traditions, believers pursue a second measure of the Holy Spirit, which is usually manifested through the exercise of certain gifts, such as tongues or prophecy.

Certainly, individual believers do experience distinct giftings from the Holy Spirit (Rom. 12:4–6), and our behavior as Christians has the potential to grieve the Holy Spirit (Eph. 4:30). Moreover, we are all exhorted to "walk by the spirit" (Gal. 5:16) and "be filled with the Spirit" (Eph. 5:18)—that is, to yield more fully to the Spirit's direction and conviction and empowerment. Yet, fundamentally, we all share in the same Holy Spirit (1 Cor. 12:11–12), and no believer possesses more of the Spirit than others do. When it comes to the presence of the Holy Spirit, then, the body of Christ is not like a commercial airplane, where there are economy, business, and first-class experiences. It is more like a big pool, where everyone swims in the same water. This is a crucial aspect of our equality and unity with one another as brothers and sisters in the Lord.

THE EMPOWERMENT OF
THE HOLY SPIRIT AND THE "SIGN GIFTS"

The second key doctrinal position that is presented in Moody's statement on the spiritual gifts involves the empowerment of the Holy Spirit. Moody believes that different spiritual gifts are given for different purposes, and this shapes our expectations for how the Holy Spirit's empowerment will be manifested within the church today. The relevant part of the statement reads as follows:

> Moody also distinguishes between spiritual gifts distributed to believers to equip them for ministry and the "sign gifts" which are understood to have been manifestations of the Holy Spirit to authenticate the messenger and the gospel message during the foundational period of the church. Therefore, Moody holds that "sign gifts" are not normative for the church today.

On the one hand, many passages of Scripture teach that the Holy Spirit gives various gifts to individual believers to equip them for the work of ministry for the sake of the whole church. For example, passages such as 1 Corinthians 12 and Ephesians 4:7–13 use the vivid analogy of a physical body to explain God's wisdom in the diversity of gifts that are given by the Holy Spirit for the building up of Christ's body.

The image is powerful: God has designed the physical body in such a way that each part has a distinct function. The hands and feet and eyes and ears each make their unique contribution, allowing us to touch and walk and see and hear. Each part is indispensable to the proper functioning of the whole body. In the same way, God has designed the body of Christ to function properly only when all of its members are making their unique contribution according to the gifting that has been given particularly to them by the Holy Spirit. Not every member will have the same gift, but rather God has given a diversity of gifts to the individual members of the church for the building up of the whole church body (1 Peter 4:10–11).

Within the passages of Scripture that describe the exercise of spiritual gifts within a church context, this work of building up the body of Christ is the purpose of the spiritual gifts that is expressed most often. However, there are also indications within Scripture that some spiritual gifts were given for a different purpose—namely, to authenticate the gospel message and its witnesses in the special circumstances of the foundational era of the church's existence. At Moody, we refer to these gifts as the "sign gifts," and we see a distinction between these gifts and the spiritual gifts that were given primarily for the purpose of building up the body of Christ for the work of ministry.[1]

Consider the uniqueness of the situation for the first generation of Christian leaders in the time period immediately following Jesus' resurrection and ascension and the outpouring of the Holy Spirit: When Jesus' first disciples began to follow Jesus' Great Commission to make disciples of all nations, it was a unique era within the history of the church. The scriptural texts that comprise the New Testament had not yet been written. The good news of the gospel was a new and audacious declaration everywhere that it was proclaimed, as Jesus' followers went out preaching that Jesus was the long-awaited Messiah who had initiated a new era in God's work in salvation history. In these special circumstances, it makes sense that God gave certain gifts as a sign to authenticate the novel message of the gospel and its witnesses.

Thus, in the book of Acts, a very select group of foundational Christian leaders is depicted as regularly performing signs and wonders as they bring the gospel to new frontiers. The only people who regularly perform signs and wonders in Acts are Peter and the Jerusalem apostles (Acts 5:12), Paul and Barnabas (Acts 14:3), and Stephen and Philip (Acts 6:8; 8:6), two of the seven men appointed as special leaders in the first generation of the Jerusalem church. These leaders perform signs and wonders at crucial stages in the advancement of the gospel, as the Christian movement expands from a small group of Jewish disciples in Jerusalem to an international, multiethnic community of Jew and Gentile believers scattered throughout the Mediterranean world.

Within the context of Acts, signs and wonders serve the purpose of authenticating the message and authority of the foundational Christian leaders who perform them. In Acts 14:1–3, for example, Paul and Barnabas are found preaching the gospel at the Jewish synagogue in Iconium. The narrator observes in verse 3, "Therefore they spent a long time there speaking boldly with reliance upon the Lord, who was testifying to the word of His grace, granting that signs and wonders be done by their hands." In other words, the signs and wonders were God's way of validating the preaching ministry of Paul and Barnabas at a foundational stage in the church's history.

Similarly, the manifestation of tongues in Acts tends to coincide with pivotal moments in which the Holy Spirit's presence is being experienced for the first time by a given group of people (Acts 2:3–4; 10:46; 19:6). The experience is not typical for every new believer throughout Acts. Rather, tongues occurs at specific transitional points in the growth of the church to validate the ethnic and geographic expansion of the Christian movement during the unique foundational era of the church's history.

Today, however, the foundational era of the apostles has passed, and in most parts of the world the church finds itself conducting its mission in circumstances that are very different from the setting of Jesus' first disciples. The Scriptures that comprise the New Testament have been written. In many places, there is an established church presence whose community life can authenticate its proclamation of the gospel. Thus, God most often fulfills the intended goal of the "sign gifts" through other means—namely, the self-authenticating Word of God and the communal witness of the church.

For this reason, Moody believes that the "sign gifts" are not normative for the church today. By this we mean that the manifestation of the "sign gifts" is not the norm or standard for how the Spirit exercises His empowerment in the church at this point in time.

Moody's position regarding the sign gifts can be distinguished from other Christian perspectives toward the spiritual gifts. At one end of the spectrum, some Christians, particularly within some Pentecostal traditions, understand the sign gifts to be normative for today in more or less complete continuity with the apostolic era. This is often what is meant whenever people refer to a "continuationist" perspective toward the spiritual gifts. At the other end of the spectrum, some Christians are convinced that the sign gifts have ceased to exist altogether. This is often labeled a "cessationist" perspective toward the gifts.

In distinction from the continuationist perspective, Moody denies that the sign gifts are normative for today. In distinction from the cessationist perspective, Moody does not take an institutional position as to whether the sign gifts now cease to exist.

There is one scriptural text in particular that historically has been central to discussions regarding whether the sign gifts exist today. In 1 Corinthians 13:8–10, Paul contrasts the permanence of love with the transient nature of gifts such as prophecy, tongues, and knowledge. Paul then states, "For we know in part and we prophesy in part; but when the perfect comes, the partial will be done away" (1 Cor. 13:9–10). The passage seems to suggest that the gifts of prophecy, tongues, and knowledge are temporary and will cease whenever the "perfect" arrives. Cessationists believe that this is a reference to the anticipated completion of the New Testament canon, so that the gifts of prophecy, tongues, and knowledge have already ceased to exist in light of the completion of the New Testament. Alternatively, many noncessationist interpreters are convinced that the "perfect" is better understood as a reference to the consummation of the ages at the second coming of Christ, so that the passage does not clearly support a cessationist perspective toward the gifts of tongues, prophecy, and knowledge.

What is clear within the broader context of 1 Corinthians is the priority and preeminence of love. How easy it is to equate spiritual gifting with spiritual maturity! When a person at church is gifted in highly visible ways, it is often natural to observe their gifts and suppose that they must be a model of spiritual maturity. Yet the magnitude or visibility of your gifting is not the true measure of your spirituality. Rather, the love of God, expressed in the mundane actions of life in Christian community, is what truly matters. That is Paul's main point in 1 Corinthians 13, whatever the passage might secondarily tell us about the present existence of the sign gifts.

Moody's statement on the spiritual gifts concludes by describing some parameters for how our position on the spiritual gifts practically finds expression in our community life at Moody: "While this institutional position is not and must not be a test of fellowship with those whose traditions differ, members of this community will not practice or propagate practices at variance with Moody's position."

Genuine, mature Christians do hold conflicting opinions about the work and gifting of the Holy Spirit. For the sake of institutional unity and consistency, we believe it is necessary for members of the Moody community not to "practice or propagate" alternative approaches to this aspect of the Christian life, yet we joyfully fellowship with brothers and sisters in Christ who do not understand or seek to experience the spiritual gifts in the same way that we do. Indeed, it is the Spirit's presence that unifies the wonderfully diverse members of God's family, creating in us a bond that transcends the differences that would otherwise break our fellowship, even when it comes to this very issue of the Holy Spirit's presence and empowerment.

ON GENDER ROLES

Laurie Norris

Moody values the worth and dignity of all persons without distinction as created in God's image. We affirm the priesthood of all believers and the responsibility of every Christian woman and man to take an active role in edifying the church. For that purpose, the Holy Spirit distributes ministry gifts to believers without distinction of any kind. That reality imposes the responsibility on every believer to fulfill ministry consistent with God's grace.

Moody distinguishes between ministry function and church office. While upholding the necessity of mutual respect and affirmation as those subject to the Word of God, Moody understands that the biblical office of elder/pastor in the early church was gender specific. Therefore, it maintains that it is consistent with that understanding of Scripture that those church offices should be limited to the male gender.

One of the most beautiful aspects of God's creation is His wise division of the human race into two genders. Males and females both have important roles to play in God's plan. Of course, in a sinful world, the oppression of women happens far too often. Many cultures have, and still do, make this a regular practice. Although it sometimes takes the form of physical abuse, it often manifests itself in more subtle ways, in which women are treated as inferior to men in worth or value. This misses what God intended. His plan is for the two genders to work together harmoniously in all spheres of human life, including in the ministries of the local church.

As important as gender roles are, however, we should note that the Doctrinal Statement of Moody Bible Institute gives secondary status to this issue. There are five main articles of core doctrine: the Trinity, the Scriptures, Christology, Anthropology, and Ecclesiology. The question of gender roles is a secondary doctrinal issue; although of course, its implications are very important in modern society. We should also note that in this chapter we are talking only about *ministry* roles. The function of women in other areas—including in the home or within a marriage—is not addressed in Moody's addendum on gender roles.

SUMMARY OF THE STATEMENT AND SCRIPTURAL EXPLANATION

Moody's doctrinal position concerning gender roles in ministry begins with an enthusiastic affirmation of the value and dignity of all persons, whether male or female. Based on God's own self-declaration at creation, we recognize the inherent value of every human being as an image bearer. Genesis 1:26–27 says, "Then God said, 'Let Us make man in Our image, according to Our likeness; and let them rule over the fish of the sea and over the birds of the sky and over the cattle and over all the earth, and over every creeping thing that creeps on the earth.' God created man in His own image, in the image of God He created him; male and female He created them." The shared divine image leads to a shared mandate for both the man and the woman, cooperating equally, to populate the earth and rule over the rest of creation as God's representatives. God's creation of the man and the woman as His image bearers reflects both their unity and their diversity, which is an inherent feature of the holy Trinity. Thus, the very first chapter of Scripture grounds gender identity in the image of God Himself. Further along in Genesis, we read that the image of God is sacred and inviolable (9:6). Bearing the divine image is one of the most fundamental aspects of being human.

At the broadest level of our shared humanity, then, both men and women possess equal worth, dignity, and responsibility as image bearers. However, there is a second affirmation in the Doctrinal Statement: the "priesthood of all believers." While this designation originally described Israel as a "kingdom of priests" who mediated the knowledge of God among the nations, we might say that the people of God in Christ Jesus have a new mandate: as Jesus Christ perfectly revealed the Father, so now the body of Christ reveals and represents Him in this world. Everyone who is "in Christ" has been indwelled by the Spirit, who joins us to our Lord and to the other members of His body (the church) with whom we enjoy union.

As the church grows in unity, so the image of Christ becomes more clearly reflected. This reflection of Christ's image has no gender distinction. Just as our Lord embodies, fulfills, and redeems true humanity, so also men and women in the church reflect the image of Christ. Every believer, indwelled by the Spirit of God in Christ, is a "priest" with a ministry function to carry out. First Peter 2:5 says that believers "are being built up as a spiritual house for a holy priesthood, to offer up spiritual sacrifices acceptable to God through Jesus Christ." Verse 9 goes on to say that just as Israel had previously functioned in a priestly role, so the church is a "royal priesthood." What an amazing privilege this is! It even caused the apostle John to burst into worshipful praise: "To Him be the glory and the dominion forever and ever! Amen" (Rev. 1:6).

Scripture could not be clearer in affirming the importance of *all* believers serving God's church—both men and women alike. Romans 12:4–8 uses body imagery to describe the orderly function of the many parts as they cooperate to make the organism stronger. First Corinthians 14:12 urges us to be "zealous" and to "seek to abound for the edification of the church." Ephesians 4:11–13 reminds us that when Christians serve each other well, the body becomes a "mature man," worthy of the "stature which belongs to the fullness of Christ."

These three passages all emphasize the centrality of spiritual gifts for the body's edification. For this reason, Moody's Doctrinal Statement points out that the priestly ministry of believers is empowered by the gifts that God bestows. The indwelling Holy Spirit enables, equips, and empowers the members of Christ's body to do His work in the world. He does this by giving gifts to each believer so we can teach and encourage the church, promote unity within the church, and carry out the practical ministry of the church.

Note that the gifts of the Spirit are given *for the church* (not for the promotion of personal status, which was the problem among believers in Corinth). As in the human body, so in Christ's mystical body, there is a beautiful harmony. And yet this one body is comprised of many members who each contribute to its life and health in various ways. The Spirit distributes these gifts without discrimination, according to the measure of His grace. Such grace "was given to each one of us according to the measure of Christ's gift" (Eph. 4:7 ESV). This verse does not say the gifts were given "to men," but "to each one of us."

Likewise, 1 Corinthians 12 and 1 Peter 4:10–11 describe the gifts as belonging to everyone in the church. Paul uses the language of gifts being bestowed "to one" and "to another," while Peter speaks similarly: "each one has received a special gift." This is precisely why the Doctrinal Statement insists that the spiritual gifts are given "without distinction of any kind." Each member of Christ's body—male and female alike—must diligently and eagerly steward these gifts, without competition or comparison, for the maturity and unity of the church. Only in this way will the body fully reflect its head, the Lord Jesus Christ.

But while the gifts belong to men and women alike, notice what the Doctrinal Statement goes on to say, "Moody distinguishes between ministry function and church office." In other words, though the spiritual gifts imparted to the members of Christ's body reflect various avenues of service within the church, they are not linked to particular church offices. Spiritual gifts are given to all members of the church, not just the clergy, for the ongoing expansion of Christ's work. Everyone must serve the purposes of God, though not necessarily by holding the same formal positions.

For example, not everyone with a gift of teaching will hold the office of elder. Not everyone with a shepherding gift will hold a formal position of authority and accountability over the flock. Not everyone with a gift of serving will serve as a deacon. So then, while everyone who holds an office in the church will have spiritual gifts, the opposite is not necessarily true: that a gifted person will necessarily hold a corresponding office. After all, there is a limited number of offices to fill. The identification of various giftings in the New Testament does not require their exercise within a particular context, nor while occupying a particular office.

Let us also remember that the biblical context for gender roles in ministry is not striving after personal gain, but sacrificial love and mutual submission. Too often, our modern culture frames the issue in terms of power dynamics. But the Doctrinal Statement reminds us of "the necessity of mutual respect and affirmation as those subject to the Word of God." Specifically, we are directed to Ephesians 5:17–21, where Paul gives us a lovely picture of believers singing hymns together in corporate worship, offering thanksgiving to God, and being subject to one another—men to women, and women to men—in "the fear of Christ."

And yet, under the banner of our mutual submission to one another—which is always a function of our ultimate submission to the Spirit of Christ—we must also affirm a divine order among human relationships, one that is rooted in creation and reflects the very character of God. Though the spiritual gifts are distributed without gender qualifications, the Bible does establish certain guidelines for those who hold the office of elder/overseer within the local church congregation. The Doctrinal Statement highlights this important fact by stating very clearly, "Moody understands that *the biblical office of elder/pastor* in the early church was gender specific. Therefore, it maintains that it is consistent with that understanding of Scripture that those church offices *should be limited to the male gender*" (italics mine). Many people today encounter a statement like this and can hear it only in terms of exclusion and oppression. Nothing could be further from the truth. When we examine the biblical basis of this affirmation, we actually find it to be a beautiful truth from the Lord. Let us look at some key texts.

First Timothy 3:1–7 describes the character of a godly elder. Among other things, he is to be peaceful, gentle, prudent, respectable, and hospitable. In the same vein, Titus 1:5–9 uses similar language to describe a man of high character. He is not quick tempered, but sensible, just, and devout. In addition to these noble qualifications, both passages emphasize that an elder must be "the husband of one wife." In other words, these two passages assume that the local church elder is male. The Greek word here is *aner*, which means a "man," or more specifically, a "husband." This does not mean that elders must be married, but only that when they are married, they are to be faithful to "one wife." As we examine the qualifications for elders, we find that the bar is set very high. Not only in marital fidelity, but in many other manifestations of virtue, elders are to be shining examples of godliness. Their gentle, protective care of the local church is a beautiful thing—never domineering, but instead carried out in love.

These two passages are further illumined by the significant discussion in 1 Timothy 2:11–12 (though this text is not cited in the Doctrinal Statement). Because of its importance, the passage is worth quoting here: "A woman must quietly receive instruction with entire submissiveness. But I do not allow a woman to teach or exercise authority over a man, but to remain quiet." Much has been written on this text in scholarly literature, and this is not the place to rehash that complicated exegetical debate. What I wish to emphasize is this: Paul clearly is talking about *the New Testament office of elder or overseer* in the local church. When he uses the phrase "to teach or exercise authority over a man," he is referring to the same person—one who teaches and has authority. In this context, such authority refers to the office of elder, whose qualifications Paul immediately goes on to delineate. The man who occupies this office is responsible for safeguarding the doctrine of the local church.

Therefore, 1 Timothy 2 is not a prohibition against a woman ever teaching biblical or theological content to a man. Consider, for example, that Priscilla, along with her husband, instructed Apollos in the "way of God" (Acts 18:26). The specific prohibition here is women being local church elders. That is why Moody Bible Institute teaches that elders "should be limited to the male gender."

EVANGELICAL POSITIONS
ON GENDER ROLES IN MINISTRY

Broadly speaking, there are two main positions held by evangelicals when it comes to the roles of men and women in Christian ministry. The first is called *complementarianism*. It argues that men and women have complementary roles to play, each distinct and each making the other more effective for the Lord's service. This is the view of Moody Bible Institute. (Though the Doctrinal Statement does not formally use such terminology, the content of this article clearly expresses a complementarian perspective.) Its theological basis is often drawn from an analogy to the doctrine of the Trinity. Each divine person of the Trinity—Father, Son, and Holy Spirit—is equal in glory, power, and fundamental essence (this is called "ontological" equality). Yet the persons of the Trinity also play distinct roles. For example, the Father does not become incarnate to die on the cross, for this work belongs only to the Son. Just as Jesus obeys the Father's will yet is in no way inferior to God the Father, so, the complementarian will argue, women and men are equal but sometimes have distinct roles to play in God's holy design.

The second position is called *egalitarianism*. This word means "equal," and the position claims (among other things) that women and men are equal in terms of what kind of ministry they can pursue in church settings. An important verse for egalitarians is Galatians 3:28: "There is neither male nor female; for you are all one in Christ Jesus." While biblical complementarians certainly agree that women are equal to men in abilities and dignity before God, the egalitarian position argues for something more: total equality in church *roles* as well. This goes beyond ontological equality to argue for a roles-based equivalence of the genders. Therefore, egalitarians hold that both women and men can be senior pastors and elders. As we have just seen, this particular teaching is not congruent with Moody's position on gender roles in ministry. However, many affirmations of the egalitarian view are fully compatible with a (biblical) complementarian perspective.

Although the debate about these two views is complicated, and there are important cultural assumptions of the ancient world that may not apply to modern times, Moody Bible Institute believes that Scripture's teaching on this matter is sufficiently clear. Cultural differences of ancient times do not *de facto* provide adequate warrant to set aside explicit biblical affirmations or prohibitions (for there is always a "cultural background" to assess in every text). Since "the biblical office of elder/pastor in the early church was gender specific," so we should follow the same pattern today.

SIGNIFICANCE OF THE DOCTRINE

As we assess the meaning of the complementarian view of gender roles in ministry, the most basic takeaway is that the local church elder, and/or the senior pastor, should be male. However, the exact meaning of this doctrine for other church roles must be considered on a case-by-case basis among different congregations—with contextual sensitivity, wisdom, and Christian charity—for Scripture does not precisely address this.

Furthermore, we should note that the Doctrinal Statement limits one thing and one thing only: the office of elder/overseer. When it comes to other ways women might serve in ministry, there are many diverse and important roles to play. For example, Moody's statement does not address:

- Women's leadership and teaching in settings not governed by local church polity, such as within educational or parachurch institutions and gatherings

- Women exercising their gifting apart from church office, such as teaching, preaching, or shepherding in settings where they would not be functioning as elders

- Women's role in the home (although complementarianism affirms the concept of male headship within marriage, the Doctrinal Statement does not address the practical outworkings of this theological commitment, as spouses live out their mutual submission under the Lord)

In today's world, the so-called "battle of the sexes" regrettably rages on with unabated fury. Against the destructive force of these cultural dynamics, which are rooted in power and competition, Scripture redemptively calls us to something higher and better. The doctrine of complementarianism leads to the flourishing of women and enables their valuable service to the church of Jesus Christ. Although local church elders are intended to be male, all gifts of the Spirit are distributed to both genders alike. Instead of focusing on one perceived limitation, let us focus instead on the enthusiastic affirmation and broadest possible application of these gifts for the good of the church. At Moody Bible Institute, the wholehearted training of women for service to Christ's kingdom—alongside their brothers who are similarly called—is one of the most beautiful ways that the gospel redirects and redeems the assumptions of the world toward the greater glory of God.

ON HUMAN SEXUALITY

Michael McDuffee

Moody's foundation for understanding human sexuality is rooted in our commitment to the Bible as the only authoritative guide for faith and practice. The first two chapters of Genesis constitute the paradigm and prerequisite for God's creative intent for human personhood, gender and sexual identity, and sexual intimacy in marriage.

THE INTENT AND THE IMPLICATIONS OF THE STATEMENT

In the beginning, the one, true triune God, who alone is sovereign and good, created the heavens and the earth. He created one man and one woman, both in His image, as the first married couple. He charged them to be fruitful and multiply. He commanded them to be caretakers of His creation. Their continued spiritual contentment and security in the presence of God was contingent upon their obeying His command not to eat from the tree of the knowledge of good and evil. Their descendants, the generations of image bearers to come, were to follow this one pattern of marriage. As God looked at this part of the creation He made, He pronounced this alluring poetry of physical sexuality as very good (Gen. 1–2). Every husband to be was to leave his father and mother to cleave to his one wife. God Himself exclusively sealed our sexuality within this primal binary bond between one male and one female. The Bible teaches God desires that each child should grow up in a home with both a father and a mother. As God designed the family, a man leaves his family of birth raised by a father and mother, to form with his wife the marriage bond that provides the same kind of family for their children (Gen. 2:24).

As the descendants of Adam and Eve, to this day, we bear that image of God (*imago Dei*) before God and all His creation, before all the angels that worship Him, before Satan and the fallen angels, before one another, and before ourselves when we turn inward to reflect upon our self-awareness. Being an image bearer of God is neither a challenge for us nor a quest. We are image bearers of God by virtue of His sheer grace, His unselfish willingness to share His goodness with us, and His simple desire to live among us. We cannot earn this privilege, nor can we discard it. The Bible reveals that none of us can fail in *being* image bearers of God because this is His doing: "God created man in His own image, in the image of God He created him; male and female He created them" (Gen. 1:27).

Having been so created, male and female complement one another. Together as husband and wife, they create and continue human life through the generations. Together as father and mother, they instruct and teach children in the way of the fear of the Lord, in wise behavior, and in righteousness, justice, and equity (Prov. 1:1–7). The Bible teaches us image bearers that God wants our sexual behavior consummated and celebrated only within a lifelong covenant of marriage between one husband and one wife (Heb. 13:4; John 2:1–11).

He has also created us to fit perfectly in a relationship with

Him. He wants to give us eternal life through Jesus Christ, the Son of God (John 17:1–3). He wants us to behold the glory He has given His Son for all eternity and to have in us the very same love with which He loves the Son (John 17:24–26). This eternal relationship defines our purpose and worth. He has made us in His image, such that we are uniquely qualified to enjoy eternal life with Him. He wants us, as His image bearers joined with Him in this special relationship, to know Him, one another, and ourselves only through His love.

Beholding the beauty of God, however, was lost in the fall of humankind into sin. The Bible tells us that Satan deceived Eve, that she ate of the fruit of the forbidden tree and gave the fruit to Adam, and that he also ate and disobeyed God. Thus, sin entered the world through satanic deception, resulting in the disobedience of man, and death entered the world through sin (Rom. 5:12). As image bearers of God, we are children of Eve, and each of us is born into Adam's original sin of disobedience. This is not a myth or a make-pretend story empty of a real historical moment. The events recorded in the first three chapters of Genesis actually happened. Myths as products of the fallen human imagination pass from one generation to the next. They are but dim memories of the works of God that distort His nature or outright deny His presence.

THE MISAPPLICATION AND MISREPRESENTATION OF THE BIBLICAL STANDARD IN CONTEMPORARY SOCIETY

A very powerful myth at work in our lives today is that of so-called sexual freedom. Its advocates assure us that taking this story to be true will result in us living fuller, more satisfying lives. We know this cannot be true because it contradicts the

Bible; it tells us to behave badly and believe false ideas. We also know legally legitimizing this lie by making it our culturally authoritative standard will cause much harm. It will destabilize the family, casting it into what social observer Mary Eberstadt calls a "state of permanent reinvention."[1]

This is really a myth of hyperindividualism, and it manifests as sexual disobedience, preying upon us by convincing us to trust in our feelings in our search for self-discovery and our seeking the good life. The careerists and entrepreneurs advancing this myth promise boys and girls and coming generations that they will enjoy life to the fullest and become who they really are if, and only if, they follow their inner sexual feelings as the true index of their identity. They encourage young people to custom design their sexual behavior to conform it to their sexual feelings. As the title of Al Mohler's book puts it, *We Cannot Be Silent* about the exalting and legal sanctioning of "all varieties of nonmarital sexual activity."[2] Speaking out, however, will not be without cost, and we must do so honestly and without hypocrisy.

Although controversial, there is substantial scientific data that highlight the harm caused from family settings other than one based upon the biblical pattern.[3] It should come as no surprise, then, that studies concluding that children suffer psychological harm when raised by homosexual parents are controversial as well.[4] Still, God has set us in a moment when we cannot rely upon the scientific community or educational institutions to support the biblical truths about human sexuality. Many modern plausibility structures[5] (or systems of meaning) in place at this time approve sexual disobedience as appropriate and normative behavior. Indeed, as the circle of acceptable sexual behavior continues to expand, many so-called keepers of legitimate knowledge today say that the deviants are the ones who challenge that expansion. Many scientific, educational, and legal experts sanction this new sexual ethic as obviously true and stigmatize anyone who proclaims the biblical definition of marriage and defends it by authority of God's Word.

We may expect that the proclaiming of the gospel under such circumstances increasingly will result in suffering ostracism: being subject to prejudice, discrimination, and exclusion. Thankfully, the Scriptures prepare us for this, teaching us that "all who desire to live godly in Christ Jesus will be persecuted" (2 Tim. 3:12). We must trust in the Holy Spirit to proclaim the gospel in public without compromise. We must put away any hypocrisy of calling for sexual purity while living sexually sinful lives. We must trust the Holy Spirit to lead us in living godly lives of sexual integrity, and as necessary, for the godly sorrow leading to repentance and confession of our sexual sins (2 Cor. 7:10).

This however, is not enough. God has placed us in a moment driven by a moral understanding that philosopher Charles Taylor calls "the ethics of authenticity."[6] This moral ideal insists we rely upon our own inner feelings as the surest source for choosing what is right. This ethic teaches me that I am to be "true to my own originality," which "is something only I can articulate and discover."[7] The Bible rejects this moral teaching. Scripture tells us, "Every man's way is right in his own eyes, but the LORD weighs the hearts" (Prov. 21:2). We are not to trust in our own heart (28:26) or depend upon our own understanding (3:5). The Scriptures tell us, "The heart is more deceitful than all else and is desperately sick" (Jer. 17:9). Although the subjective sense of authenticity seems right to many today, it is the way of death (Prov. 14:12; 16:25). Whatever the cost, we must proclaim these truths, also insisting that God loves all those who endorse sexual disobedience, as well as all those convinced and conditioned to participate in it. These men, women, and children are all image bearers of God. God created them so they might "enter into a relationship with their creator," and "to represent [Him] on earth and rule as His regents under Him."[8] They both approve and live immoral lives, but He neither abandons them nor leaves them unloved.

In proclaiming this truth, it is crucial that we remove any unnecessary obstacles that might inhibit the deceived and disobedient from hearing about God's love for them. We cannot hide our sins of the past. We must be honest and transparent. This is especially the case in how Christians in the past used the Bible to stigmatize people as inferior simply owing to the color of their skin, even to the point of writing and defending racist laws that prohibited interracial sex and marriage. Happily for our country, these laws have since been overturned, ultimately in the 1967 US Supreme Court decision *Loving v. Virginia*.[9]

This precedent regarding race is the basis of a similar demand for the legalization and legitimization of same-sex marriage, affirmed by the US Supreme Court in *Obergefell v. Hodges* (2015).[10] We face an approaching deluge of demands for the legalization of even wider sexual self-indulgence. The year 2018 marks when for "the first time in any court, a federal judge . . . has ruled that transgender people are entitled to the fullest protection of the Constitution against discrimination."[11] Educational institutions instruct the impressionable that our sex is an assigned label based on the genitals with which we are born, while gender is a set of social expectations. Scientists and educators deceive parents and children into believing we base our gender identity upon how we feel inside. *Transgender*, for example, describes a person whose gender identity—feeling inside as male, female, both, or none of these—does not match the biological sex assigned at birth. Sexual orientation, they further inform us, is our feeling of attraction toward others. "A person may be attracted to people of the same sex, of the opposite sex, or without reference to sex or gender. Some people do not experience sexual attraction and may identify as asexual." Children and adolescents learn their feelings about gender identity and sexual orientation may change. "Many folks, old and young, experience changes in who they're attracted to and how they identify. This is called 'fluidity.'"[12]

The present-day false prophets promising we flourish best through pursuit of sexual liberties are unleashing a legal nightmare on future generations. They threaten the social stability that depends upon the order of marriage, which God Himself created and sanctioned. As evangelicals, we must urge men, women, and children to listen to Jesus, who endorsed that created order and said, "What therefore God has joined together, let no man separate" (Matt. 19:6; Mark 10:9). We must remind them that marriage is so important to God that the Bible likens it to the union between Christ and His church (Eph. 5:22–33).

We must also warn them that what Charles Taylor calls the immanent frame of exclusive humanism[13] does not describe the totality of our lives. God is eternal (1 Tim. 1:17) and His lovingkindness is everlasting (Ps. 136). He has created us to enjoy eternal life in His presence (Rev. 22:3–5). The shortness of temporal life and the shorter chapter still within it marked by our potential for sexual activity does not begin to measure who we are in the fullness of God's free gift of eternal life in Christ Jesus our Lord. Reflection upon these truths revealed in the Word of righteousness guards us from dullness of hearing into which the gravitational pull of the sexual seeks to draw us (1 Cor. 4:16–18; 5:1–8; Heb. 5:13–14).

No matter the resistance or ridicule we may face, we must teach that the Bible sets the boundaries of our behavior—sexual and otherwise. With passionate determination, we must strive to help others understand that our most essential characteristic, whether we are boys and girls or men and women, is that each of us is an image bearer of God. We must preach the gospel, shouting from the rooftops that God loves us and wants only good for us, and we should trust Him for it.

Today, even now, God demonstrates His own love toward us in that while we were yet sinners, Christ died for us (Rom. 5:8). All of us suffer the corruption, frustration, anxiety, and shame of sin. Whatever nebula of feelings swirl inside of us at any given moment, none communicates to us who we truly are. Jesus Christ died our death to sin on the cross for us. God raised Him from the dead, putting an end to the agony of death, since it was impossible for Jesus to be held in its power (Acts 2:24). God invites each of us to look to Jesus, the perfect image bearer of God and to believe in Him for the forgiveness of sin and for receiving the gift of eternal life. We need to believe "in the testimony that God has given concerning His Son. And the testimony is this, that God has given us eternal life, and this life is in His Son. He who has the Son has the life; he who does not have the Son of God does not have the life" (1 John 5:10–12). Jesus lives and saves forever whoever believes in Him. Knowing today is the day of salvation, let us urge one another, whether single or married, to live chaste lives. Let us together trust in the Holy Spirit to give as our strength the joy of the Father so we might live in the likeness of Jesus. Today Jesus listens to us; today He helps us. For He Himself has said, "I will never desert you, nor will I ever forsake you" (Heb. 13:5), and "Lo, I am with you always, even to the end of the age" (Matt. 28:20).

MOVING FORWARD WITH STEADFAST, HUMBLE CONVICTION

John A. Jelinek

In reality, everyone *is* a theologian—of one sort or another. And therein lies the problem. There is nothing wrong with being an amateur theologian or a professional theologian, but there is everything wrong about being an ignorant or a sloppy theologian.[1]

Ten years ago, when I began working at Moody Bible Institute, a colleague was showing me how to navigate the city of Chicago. He took me to the intersection of Madison and State, and explained that, since 1909, all streets in Chicago are defined in relation to this single intersection as the base reference point and that I need never get lost if I would remember and apply this fact to the numbers and directions of the street signs of Chicago. Streets have changed since 1909, but that reference point in Chicago has remained constant. Over the past ten years, that tutorial has served me well in navigating the city. I always know where I am in relation to that reference point.

Carefully crafted articulations of biblical teachings serve Christians in a way similar to the ways people apply common knowledge of that Chicago city intersection. Doctrinal clarity can help us navigate and know not only where we must stand in affirming orthodoxy, but also where others stand in relation to our own beliefs about what the Bible teaches. The teachings of the Bible, because it *is* God's Word, do not change with the culture. What does change about doctrine is how individual theologians, whether amateur or professional, imperfectly or accurately express their understanding of how those doctrines may be expressed in their respective generations and in diverse cultures.

Perhaps this is why a wide array of theological options exist in the world of contemporary theology, including both Protestant and evangelical contemporary theology. The discerning reader of contemporary theologies will, therefore, read critically. In modern expressions of theology, diversity of opinion can be perceived even in some of the basic and foundational subjects of theology addressed in this volume. Sorting out the options requires sorting presuppositions and priorities—and, ultimately, recognizing where authority resides.

Good theologians recognize the factor of the authority of the God who stands behind His Word. They wrestle with both the message of the Bible and all its attendant implications. Because they view God as its source, they recognize that what God says is, by virtue of His nature, inerrant. We recognize that there was human involvement in the process,[2] but such involvement does not *require* that error resulted. We also believe that the teachings of the Bible can be integrated and harmonized; that a systematization of biblical teachings is possible as a corollary of inerrancy. There is little point in trying to harmonize the teachings of an errant Scripture, but much profit and benefit to the church results when God's inerrant Word is endorsed and we speak its harmonious message!

Some people mistakenly look at a particular doctrinal statement as though such a statement was *the* fixed and authoritative reference point. Moody faculty members subscribe to the Institute's Doctrinal Statement without reservation and believe that authority belongs solely to God who revealed unchanging truth through His words in the words of the original manuscripts of Scripture. In accord with historic Protestant faith, and in accordance with the historic Reformation doctrine of *Sola Scriptura*, we consider the Scriptures not only as sufficient, but also as our supreme authority in all spiritual matters.

A while ago, a faculty colleague was discussing his discipline with me and getting into some rather difficult technical and theological issues, seeking my opinion as a theologian. At length, he paused and said, "You should be grateful that you teach Bible and theology. The facts of your discipline are static. Theology never changes." I was taken aback at his statement at first, but realized that he was really affirming what is said above: that absolute truths in Scripture do not change to become untrue with the passing of time. In many disciplines, what is given today as a universally accepted truth may change tomorrow when a contravening of consensus facts are uncovered. Whatever is affirmed in Scripture does not change, though our understanding of such is imperfect. The world, however, and its perspectives on reality and truth are constantly changing, and that is one point behind our fuller exposition of the MBI Doctrinal Statement.

Doctrinal statements define parameters of belief for those who voluntarily subscribe to them. They divide Christians from one another at times, but in their best expressions unite Christians in important affirmations of timeless truth revealed by the one true and loving God. For MBI faculty, in all its educational endeavors, the explanations that precede this chapter are our attempt to invite others to our common understanding of biblical truth. Biblical truth is not only absolute, but also intended to be soul-nurturing and life-affirming because it proceeds from a loving God who is both transcendent and personal. Culture and perspectives change, but we need to apply biblical truth in fresh ways to situations the Bible never addresses directly. We are nourished by doctrine in order to be good ministers of Christ (1 Tim. 4:6), holding on to what we have been taught (Titus 1:9) and avoiding those who promote incorrect doctrine (Rom. 16:17). Doctrine matters because the Bible teaches that people's eternal destinies are at stake.

At MBI, we believe that what people believe about God, His Word and its authority, salvation, ethics, and the Bible ought to translate into more than just creeds and affirmations. What we know from God has implications that ought to *change us.* The purpose of theology is related to the church. Theology should teach the church about its foundation as defined by the Bible (Titus 2:1). Theology also provides perspective for understanding the wider culture and the world in which the church is located. Theology operates between the intersection of the Bible and culture. For evangelicals, the Bible always bears the emphasis in any tension on matters of dispute.

We further believe that God's Word was meant to engage our culture. The day in which we find ourselves obliges each believer to find his or her way to well-defined and resolute positions on biblical Christian teaching. These days, the church is often as much damaged by carelessness and ambiguity about matters of doctrine from within as it is beset by cynics and unbelievers without. A survey from Ligonier Ministries and LifeWay Research published in October 2018 bears this out. The survey found that of Protestant evangelicals, 78 percent strongly agree that Jesus was the first being created by God, and 59 percent believe the Holy Spirit is a spiritual force rather than a personal being. And back in 2014, 22 percent said that God the Father is "more divine" than Jesus.[3] If these surveys are representative of current theological awareness, then basic teachings of the Christian faith are misunderstood by a significant number of evangelical Christians!

For these reasons and more, Christians today need to discern and declare God's Word with both boldness and humility. We must be bold because the written Word needs also to be spoken, to be proclaimed in the words of the gospel to a biblically incompatible culture. We must be humble because we are servants who wield no authority other than that of the Word of God itself. We embrace the exegesis of the text and we also engage the exhilarating challenge of moving beyond to the exegesis of the complex and ever-changing contexts of worldly life. We seek to learn how to hear and speak God's Word amid the constant noise and distraction of merely human babble.

As Moody faculty address, in publications and in the classroom, the issues of our day in a conflicted culture, they will surely face opposition, as many people have ascribed to beliefs that collide with a biblical worldview. Some will disagree with our views on issues such as the order of events for the end times or the meaning of Romans 9–11 for the church and national Israel.[4] Others may take exception to the MBI understanding of everlasting punishment, as some theologians seek to deny the biblical teaching regarding an endless punishment in hell and rather opt for annihilationism, universalism, purgatory, or the denial of hell altogether. A theology of mission and the necessity of addressing the need for the proclamation of the gospel—including what the gospel is—are additional issues that Moody faculty could address to the profit of the church.

Topics that generate controversy today often concern our

public theology: How will we apply the Bible to contemporary ethics (our politics and civic responsibilities)? How does our faith give evidence that it is genuine? How does faith lead us to regard and love our neighbor? How does faith shape our view of systems and patterns of behavior deeply ingrained in us yet denied by certain people of power? Addressing these questions will require some forethought and redress in matters of Bible interpretation (hermeneutics and how we know what we know) to properly navigate the areas of disagreement over how Christians should engage with culture.

Such discussions may be the most challenging of all, since they raise the question of why unbelievers sometimes see problems of injustice more clearly than we or our fellow believers see them. What should our theology embrace as a reliable guide to righteous living? How could our intellectual appropriation of theological propositions better relate to our faith practices as we live out Paul's directive: "And do not be conformed to this world, but be transformed by the renewing of your mind" (Rom. 12:2)?

We cannot improve upon the enduring gospel in its proclamation of the crucified and risen Christ as the only hope for sinners.[5] But can we progress in our application of biblical truths that attend to right doctrine? As the 500th anniversary of the posting of Martin Luther's *Ninety-Five Theses* has come and gone, it is good for organizations like MBI to affirm and reaffirm commitment to biblical orthodoxy. If the Reformation *Solas*[6] are to edify believers in generations to come, it may prove helpful for our faculty to recount how believers relate to these truths today.

The church, and MBI in service to the church, should never relegate evangelism to a secondary purpose status for our existence. Other questions attend to this emphasis. How are the Bible, Christian tradition, the church, and culture weighted in their importance for evangelicals engaging theology? Historically, one major difference between Protestant and Roman Catholic theology was that Protestants insisted on the priority of the authority of the Bible (in its original autographs), whereas Roman Catholics understood the church to be the authoritative interpreter of both Christian tradition and the Bible itself. Do not these topics deserve examination and reaffirmation for the sake of the church?

A "new perspective" movement, connected with an increase of scholarly interest in studying the Bible in the context of relevant ancient texts and social-scientific methods, has arisen and called for the reinterpretation of biblical texts based on studies of the ancient world. This movement represents a significant shift since the 1960s in the way some scholars interpret Paul's writings. In Romans, Paul advocates justification through faith in Jesus Christ over justification through works of the Law (3:20–24). Reformed theologians agreed that Paul was arguing that good works do not factor into justification; only faith does. But according to this "new perspective," Paul was not addressing good works in general, but questioning only observances such as circumcision, dietary laws, and Sabbath laws. Such conclusions, if true, impact the nature of the gospel that is preached. Moving forward, standing firm may require further redress of these and attendant issues.

Finally, but not exhaustively, the traditional Christian view that salvation is found only in Jesus is being challenged everywhere. Religious pluralism allows that all religions lead to either salvation or heaven—and this mindset is becoming more popular. Intense opposition and rhetoric are directed toward Christians who espouse the exclusivity of Jesus' claims. Traditional Christian views are often linked with "hate" and "intolerance." In standing firm on its doctrines, is the MBI brand of Christian particularism or exclusivism promoting hate? How can we not respond in love to those who raise these false charges?

Historically, many Christians have looked to MBI with confidence in our reliance on the Bible. Over 40,000 alumni serving across the world have testified to the effectiveness of the biblical training they received at Moody. Looking forward, the church of Jesus Christ can have confidence that the perspective of the Moody Bible Institute will always be fixed by the counsel of the inerrant, authoritative, ever-relevant, and life-transforming Word of God.

THE MBI DOCTRINAL STATEMENT

ARTICLE I

God is triune, one Being eternally existing in three co-equal Persons: Father, Son, and Holy Spirit; these divine Persons, together possessing the same eternal perfections, work inseparably and harmoniously in creating, sustaining, and redeeming the world.

(Genesis 1; John 1:1–3; Hebrews 1:1–3; Deuteronomy 6:4; Ephesians 4:4–6; Acts 5:3–4; 1 Corinthians 8:6; 1 Timothy 2:5; John 14:9–10, 26; Matthew 28:18–19; 2 Corinthians 13:14; Revelation 4:11)

ARTICLE II

The Bible, including both the Old and the New Testaments, is a divine revelation, the original autographs of which were verbally inspired by the Holy Spirit.[1]

(2 Timothy 3:16; 2 Peter 1:21)

ARTICLE III

Jesus Christ is the image of the invisible God, which is to say, He is Himself very God; He took upon Himself our nature, being conceived by the Holy Spirit and born of the Virgin

Mary;[2] He died upon the cross as a substitutionary sacrifice for the sin of the world;[3] He arose from the dead in the body in which He was crucified; He ascended into heaven in that body glorified, where He is now our interceding High Priest; He will come again personally and visibly to set up His kingdom[4] and to judge the quick and the dead.

(Colossians 1:15; Philippians 2:5–8; Matthew 1:18–25; 1 Peter 2:24–25; Luke 24; Hebrews 4:14–16; Acts 1:9–11; 1 Thessalonians 4:16–18; Matthew 25:31–46; Revelation 11:15–17; 20:4–6, 11–15)

ARTICLE IV

Man was created[5] in the image of God but fell into sin, and, in that sense, is lost; this is true of all men, and except a man be born again he cannot see the kingdom of God; salvation is by grace through faith in Christ who His own self bore our sins in His own body on the tree; the retribution of the wicked and unbelieving and the rewards of the righteous are everlasting, and as the reward is conscious, so is the retribution.[6]

(Genesis 1:26–27; Romans 3:10, 23; John 3:3; Acts 13:38–39; 4:12; John 3:16; Matthew 25:46; 2 Corinthians 5:1; 2 Thessalonians 1:7–10)

ARTICLE V

The Church[7] is an elect company of believers baptized by the Holy Spirit into one body; its mission is to witness concerning its Head, Jesus Christ, preaching the gospel among all nations; it will be caught up to meet the Lord in the air ere He appears to set up His kingdom.[8]

(Acts 2:41; 15:13–17; Ephesians 1:3–6; 1 Corinthians 12:12–13; Matthew 28:19–20; Acts 1:6–8; 1 Thessalonians 4:16–18)

NOTES ELABORATING
UPON THE 1928 DOCTRINAL STATEMENT

1. The Bible is without error in all it affirms in the original autographs and is the only authoritative guide for faith and practice and as such must not be supplanted by any other fields of human learning.

2. Jesus Christ, the only begotten Son of God, is fully God and fully man possessing both deity and humanity united in one person, without division of the person or confusion of the two natures.

3. An individual receives the benefit of Christ's substitutionary death by faith as the result of responding to the message of the gospel. Salvation is the free gift of God's grace through faith alone, in Christ alone, therefore not dependent upon church membership, intermediaries, sacraments or works of righteousness to attain or sustain it.

4. It is Moody's position that this refers to the premillennial return of Christ at which time He will set up His millennial reign, during which time He will fulfill His promises to Israel.

5. This affirms that the first human beings were a special and unique creation by God as contrasted to being derived from any preexisting life forms. Further, God created everything "after its kind," which excludes any position that allows for any evolutionary process between kinds.

6. This statement excludes any position which asserts a temporary or complete cessation of consciousness or merging with eternal oneness or annihilation of the damned or a "second chance" or a period of suffering or purification in preparation for entrance into the presence of God.

7. The church of Jesus Christ is a distinct entity from Israel in the ongoing program of God. Further, this universal church consists of all who possess saving faith in the death and resurrection of Jesus Christ from Pentecost to the rapture of the church and which will represent every language, people and nation.

8. Christ will return in the air preceding the seven-year tribulation at which time He will receive into heaven all believers who constitute His church. During that tribulation period, God will bring salvation to Israel and the nations while exercising judgment on unbelievers.

INSTITUTIONAL POSITIONS RELATED TO THE MBI DOCTRINAL STATEMENT

In addition to the distinctive elements derived from a historic understanding of the 1928 Doctrinal Statement, Moody has historically been identified with the positions outlined below. Although trustees, education administrators, and faculty are expected to hold these positions, we recognize that we serve and minister with others whose traditions differ on these subjects.

GENDER ROLES IN MINISTRY

Moody values the worth and dignity of all persons without distinction as created in God's image. We affirm the priesthood of all believers and the responsibility of every Christian woman and man to take an active role in edifying the church. For that purpose, the Holy Spirit distributes ministry gifts to believers without distinction of any kind. That reality imposes the responsibility on every believer to fulfill ministry consistent with God's grace.

Moody distinguishes between ministry function and church office. While upholding the necessity of mutual respect and affirmation as those subject to the Word of God, Moody understands that the biblical office of elder/pastor in the early church was gender specific. Therefore, it maintains that it is consistent with that understanding of Scripture that those church offices should be limited to the male gender.

SIGN GIFTS OF THE HOLY SPIRIT

Moody maintains that there is one baptism of the Holy Spirit that occurs at the time a person is born again, placing that one into the body of Christ. Moody also distinguishes between spiritual gifts distributed to believers to equip them for ministry and the "sign gifts," which are understood to have been manifestations of the Holy Spirit to authenticate the messenger and the gospel message during the foundational period of the church. Therefore, Moody holds that "sign gifts" are not normative for the church today. While this institutional position is not and must not be a test of fellowship with those whose traditions differ, members of this community will neither practice nor propagate practices at variance with Moody's position.

HUMAN SEXUALITY

Moody's foundation for understanding human sexuality is rooted in our commitment to the Bible as the only authoritative guide for faith and practice. The first two chapters of Genesis constitute the paradigm and prerequisite for God's creative intent for human personhood, gender and sexual identity, and sexual intimacy in marriage (Genesis 1:27; 2:24; cf. Matthew 19:4–5).

We affirm that humanity came from the hand of God with only two sexual distinctions, male and female, both bearing the image of God, and emerging from one flesh with the unique physical capacity to reunite as one flesh in complementarity within a marriage. God's creation design and intent for marriage as expressed in Genesis 2 is therefore exclusively between one man and one woman. Within this monogamous context, intended to be lifelong, sexual intimacy is a glorious blessing from God.

Based on biblical theology (cf. Leviticus 18; 1 Corinthians 5–6; and other passages), we conclude that non marital sex, homosexual sex, same-sex romantic relationships, and transgender expressions are deviations from God's standard, misrepresenting the nature of God Himself. As such, these are wrong under any circumstances in God's eyes. We affirm the worth and relevance of human gender and sexuality as a distinctive of marriage. Consequently, we consider all other forms of sexual expression sinful, misaligned with God's purposes.

We affirm God's love and concern for all of humanity, a concern that compelled Him to offer His Son a ransom for our lives, and we consider His biblically recorded and specifically defined guidelines for sexual practice to be enduring expressions of His love and protection of our human identity (Matthew 19:5–9).

Our expectation is that each member of Moody's community will honor the biblical obligation to surrender one's body to God. Non marital sexual intimacy, homosexual sexual intimacy and same-sex romantic relationships, and gender identification that is incongruent with one's birth sex are all violations of biblical teaching from which Moody derives its community standards. We willingly submit ourselves to these biblical mandates in light of our call to holiness and to self-surrender.

ACKNOWLEDGMENTS

It is an exceptional privilege to have an opportunity to address not only a significant historical statement such as the Moody Doctrinal Statement, but also to speak to its application and relevance for the mission and ministries of the Moody Bible Institute today. This volume, though short in length, is the result of the talents of many people to bring it to print. As general editors, we are grateful for a collegial and knowledgeable faculty who could address the issues with brevity, grace, and perspicacity. We pray that their contributions are received in the prayerful spirit in which they are offered. For those who have attended the Institute in one of its educational programs in the past, we hope that they find confirmation of the truths they were taught and validation of those same truths through the practices of those whose words find their way onto these pages.

Our thanks also goes to our wives, Denise and Linda, who made room for our writing and editing distractions in pursuing this project alongside our abnormally busy lives together. Their support and prayer by God's grace make our ministries not only possible but pleasant (our extension of Psalm 16:6).

Thanks to Kevin Emmert for his diligence in carefully reviewing and editing the chapters, making many helpful and clarifying suggestions.

We are particularly appreciative of Greg Thornton for his unflagging support for our faculty and this project. Greg's legacy of integrity and leadership ideally suited him to step into the interim presidency of Moody during a time of upheaval and transition, and is additional evidence that God continues to bestow great riches on Moody Bible Institute through the people who lead, teach, and serve here.

Finally, we are grateful to God for the opportunity to serve at a place like Moody. To be used of God here is a great thing, especially when we come to the end of ourselves and realize that God has been the One at work in us both to will and to do according to His good pleasure (Phil. 2:13).

NOTES

The Significance of the MBI Doctrinal Statement

1. James M. Gray (author), D. B. Towner (composer), "Christian Fellowship Song" (1909), in *The Voice of Thanksgiving No. 2*, prepared by The Moody Bible Institute of Chicago, ed. D. B. Towner (New York: Fleming H. Revell Company, 1916), hymn #16, https://hymnary.org/hymn/VoT21916/16.
2. The first major split in the church that divided it between the Eastern Church centered on Constantinople, and the Western Church centered on Rome.
3. As Dr. Quiggle will demonstrate in his chapter on Moody's doctrinal history, it is clear that Mr. Moody and the early leaders of the Institute expected a future return of Jesus to set up His kingdom on earth (a key conclusion of dispensationalist hermeneutics), and that position continues to shape the Institute until the present day. While all of our contributors work from within a dispensational framework, Dr. Tucker will delve much more deeply into these matters in his discussion of the church.
4. In the spring of 2018, the Board of Trustees decided to require of itself, officers, and faculty the affirmation of the shorter statement of the Chicago Statement on Biblical Inerrancy, and the nineteen included Affirmations and Denials. In so doing, the Board expressed a desire to deepen and clarify the commitment to biblical inerrancy already included in the footnote to the second article of the doctrinal statement, and it is for that reason that Dr. Sanchez mentions the Chicago Statement in his treatment of the inerrancy and authority of Scripture.

The History of the MBI Doctrinal Statement

1. William R. Moody, *The Life of Dwight L. Moody by His Son* (New York: Fleming H. Revell Co., 1900), 107.
2. By "practical," I mean Moody was more interested in the practical matters of converting sinners and discipling converts rather than theological speculation. It is practicality within the sphere of evangelism.
3. Stanley Gundry, *Love Them In: The Proclamation Theology of D. L. Moody* (Chicago: Moody, 1976). Gundry summarizes the various theories on Moody's attitude toward theology on pages 62–70. Gundry's work is still the definitive work on Mr. Moody's theological commitments, and I am indebted to his insights.
4. Dwight Moody, *Wondrous Love* (London: J. E. Hawkins, 1875), 261–64; D. L. Moody, *Glad Tidings: Comprising Sermons and Prayer-Meeting Talks Delivered at the N. Y. Hippodrome* (New York: E. B. Treat, 1876), 270–73.

5. "Addresses delivered by Mr. D. L. Moody," General Conference, Saturday Evening, August 12, 1899, typed manuscript, Moody Bible Institute Archives, 4.
6. Moody, *Glad Tidings*, 452.
7. After Mr. Moody's death in 1899, the Board of Trustees voted to rename the school, The Moody Bible Institute of Chicago.
8. MS copy of charter, Moody Papers, Moody Bible Institute; Minutes, Board of Trustees' Meetings, Chicago Evangelization Society, handwritten extracts in Moody Papers, Moody Bible Institute, February 17, 1887. These are housed in the Legal Department of Moody Bible Institute.
9. *The Fundamentals: A Testimony to Truth* was initially a series of ninety essays published between 1910–1916 as a twelve-volume set by the Testimony Publishing Company of Chicago. The essays were eventually republished as a four-volume set in 1917 by the Bible Institute of Los Angeles, known today as Biola University. They are generally referred to as simply "The Fundamentals."
10. "Liberalism or Christianity," J. Gresham Machen, *Princeton Theological Review* vol. 20, 1923.
11. Handwritten minutes from the Board of Trustees Minutes of the Moody Bible Institute, dated December 11, 1912. Handwritten minutes from the Board of Trustees Minutes of the Moody Bible Institute, dated July 8, 1914. These are both housed in the Legal Department of Moody Bible Institute.
12. *The Christian Workers Magazine* (January 1920), vol. 20, 382, Moody Bible Institute of Chicago.
13. The text of the Doctrinal Statement of the World Conference on Christian Fundamentals 1919 can be found at https://archive.org/stream/TheDoctrinal StatementOfTheWorldConferenceOnChristianFundamentals1919/The%20 Doctrinal%20Statement%20of%20the%20World%20Conference%20 on%20Christian%20Fundamentals%201919_djvu.txt. The Statement was very influential. In fact, it served as the basis for the doctrinal statement adopted by Wheaton College in 1926.
14. Moody Bible Institute, "2018–2019 Undergraduate Catalogue," 7, https:// www.moody.edu/siteassets/website_assets/files/academic-catalogs/under graduate/ug-catalog_2018-2019.pdf.
15. The full text can be found online at https://www.moodybible.org/beliefs/ sign-gifts/.
16. The full text can be found online at https://www.moodybible.org/beliefs/ gender-roles/.
17. The full text can be found on page 12 of the 2018–2019 Undergraduate Catalogue of the Moody Bible Institute. The catalogue can be found online at https://www.moody.edu/siteassets/website_assets/files/academic-catalogs/ undergraduate/ug-catalog_2018-2019.pdf.

On the Triune God

1. See Tertullian, *Against Praxeas*, 8 in *Latin Christianity: Its Founder, Tertullian*, Ante-Nicene Fathers, vol. 3, ed. Allan Menzies (Peabody, MA: Hendrickson Publishers, 1995), 1348–49; and Athanasius, *On the Councils of Ariminum and Seleucia*, 52 in *Athanasius: Select Works and Letters*, Nicene and Post-Nicene Fathers, ser. 2, vol. 4, ed. Philip Schaff and Henry Wace (Peabody, MA: Hendrickson Publishers, 1995), 1180–81.

2. Gregory of Nyssa, "To Ablabius: On 'Not Three Gods'" in *Select Writings and Letters of Gregory, Bishop of Nyssa*, Nicene and Post-Nicene Fathers, ser. 2, vol. 5, ed. Philip Schaff and Henry Wace (Peabody, MA: Hendrickson Publishers, 1995), 623–24.

On Jesus Christ

1. See the collection of essays in *Retrieving Eternal Generation*, eds. by Fred Sanders and Scott R. Swain (Grand Rapids, MI: Zondervan, 2017).
2. See the excellent discussion in Michael J. Ovey, *"Your Will Be Done": Exploring Eternal Subordination, Divine Monarchy and Divine Humility* (London: The Latimer Trust, 2016).

On Creation and the Fall

1. The earliest evidence of the Apostles' Creed is found in a letter written by the Council of Milan in AD 390.
2. Brevard S. Childs, *Old Testament Theology in Canonical Context* (Philadelphia: Fortress, 1985), 31.
3. John Goldingay, *Biblical Theology: The God of the Christian Scriptures* (Downers Grove, IL: IVP Academic, 2016), 177; quoting James Dunn, *Theology of Paul the Apostle* (Grand Rapids, MI: William B. Eerdmans, 1998), 53.
4. Childs, *Old Testament Theology*, 31.
5. Goldingay, *Biblical Theology*, 137.
6. Anthony C. Thiselton, *Systematic Theology* (Grand Rapids, MI: Eerdmans, 2015), 102.
7. Goldingay, *Biblical Theology*, 137.
8. William J. Dumbrell, *The Search for Order: Biblical Eschatology in Focus* (Grand Rapids, MI: Baker, 1994), 22–23.
9. Childs, *Old Testament Theology*, 46.
10. Eugene H. Merrill, "Fall of Humankind," *NIDOTTE*, vol. 4, ed. W.A. VanGemeren (Grand Rapids, MI: Zondervan, 1997), 638.
11. John Kessler, *Old Testament Theology: Divine Call and Human Response* (Waco, TX: Baylor University Press, 2013), 138 n. 106.
12. Nahum M. Sarna, *The JPS Torah Commentary: Genesis* (Philadelphia: JPS, 1989), 27.
13. Gordon J. Wenham, *Genesis 1-15*, Word Biblical Commentary, vol. 1 (Waco, TX: Word, 1987), 63–64.
14. Merrill, "Fall of Humankind," 638.
15. Anthony C. Thiselton, "Sin," in *The Thiselton Companion to Christian Theology* (Grand Rapids, MI: Eerdmans, 2015), 771.

On the Church

1. "Doctrinal Statement Moody Bible Institute," https://www.moody.edu/about/our-beliefs/doctrinal-statement/.
2. "Doctrinal Statement Moody Bible Institute and Institutional Positions Related to the Moody Bible Institute Doctrinal Statement (1928)," https://www.moodybible.org/beliefs/.
3. Ibid.

4. Michael Bird, *Evangelical Theology* (Grand Rapids, MI: Zondervan, 2013), 713.

5. Acts 15:13–17 is cited in the original Moody Statement. William Marty, "Acts," in *Moody Bible Commentary*, ed. Michael Rydelnik and Michael Vanlaningham (Chicago: Moody, 2014), is helpful here: "James's citation of Amos is primarily about the inclusion of Gentiles among the people of God without their having to become Jewish, not about the restoration of David's kingdom in and through the church (as covenant theologians argue," 1706.

6. Marcus Peter Johnson, *One With Christ: An Evangelical Theology of Salvation* (Wheaton, IL: Crossway, 2013), 192–193.

7. John Frame, *Systematic Theology* (Phillipsburg, PA: P & R), 178. While Peter is the focal point here, Ephesians 2:20 makes it clear that New Testament persons are the foundation of the church: "apostles and prophets, with Christ Jesus himself as the chief cornerstone."

8. Daniel Wallace, *Greek Grammar* (Grand Rapids, MI: Zondervan, 1996), 568.

9. Walter Bauer, *A Greek English Lexicon of the New Testament and Other Early Christian Literature*, 3rd ed. (BDAG), revised and edited by Frederick William Danker (Chicago: University of Chicago Press, 2001), 303.

10. Norman Geisler, *Systematic Theology* (Minneapolis: Bethany House, 2005), 4.28.

11. J. Brian Tucker, *Reading 1 Corinthians* (Eugene, OR: Cascade Books, 2018), 83–85.

12. John MacArthur and Richard Mayhue, *Biblical Doctrine* (Wheaton, IL: Crossway, 2017), 741. See further discussion on the rapture in the chapter dealing with that topic.

13. Lewis Sperry Chafer, *Systematic Theology* (Dallas: Dallas Theological Seminary, 1948), 4.47–53. He provides a list of over twenty ways in which Israel and the church are distinct. This is not the same understanding of the new covenant community as put forth by Peter Gentry and Stephen Wellum, *Kingdom through Covenant* (Wheaton, IL: Crossway, 2012), 684–85; nor Gregg Allison, *Sojourners and Strangers* (Wheaton, IL: Crossway, 2012), 61–100.

14. Frame, *Systematic Theology*, 1018.

15. J. Brian Tucker, *Reading Romans after Supersessionism* (Eugene, OR: Cascade Books, 2018), 133. Frame also ignores the syntactical difficulties with his position, especially in relation to the use of *kai* (and or even).

16. Charles Ryrie, *Basic Theology* (Chicago: Moody, 1999), 462.

17. Michael Vlach, *He Will Reign Forever* (Silverton, OR: Lampion, 2017), 540.

18. Ibid.

19. Rolland McCune, *Systematic Theology* (Allen Park, MI: Detroit Baptist Theological Seminary, 2010), 3.203. The two-program approach is central to premillennial Dispensational readings. See Robert Lightner, "The Nature and Purpose of the Church," in *The Fundamentals for the Twenty-First Century*, ed. Mal Couch (Grand Rapids, MI: Kregel, 2000), 323–38, here 324.

20. See Robert Saucy, *The Church in God's Program* (Chicago: Moody, 1972), 69–97; J. Brian Tucker and John Koessler, *All Together Different* (Chicago: Moody, 2018), 109–52; Craig Blaising and Darrell Bock, *Progressive Dispensationalism* (Wheaton, IL: BridgePoint, 1993).

On the Last Things

1. Such is attested by a recent surge of scholarship on the topic. For example, see James M. Scott, ed., *Restoration: Old Testament, Jewish, and Christian Perspectives* (Leiden, Netherlands: Brill, 2001); Darrell L. Bock and Mitch Glaser, eds., *The People, the Land, and the Future of Israel: Israel and the Jewish People in the Plan of God* (Grand Rapids, MI: Kregel, 2014); Gerald R. McDermott, ed., *The New Christian Zionism: Fresh Perspectives on Israel and the Land* (Downers Grove, IL: IVP Academic, 2016).

2. In addition to the relevant essays in the edited volumes listed in note 1, see David Ravens, *Luke and the Restoration of Israel* (JSNTSup 119; Sheffield, UK: Sheffield Academic Press, 1995); Christoph Schaefer, *Die Zukunft Israels bei Lukas: Biblisch-frühjüdische Zukunftsvorstellungen im lukanischen Doppelwerk im Vergleich zu Röm 9-11* (BZNW 190; Berlin: de Gruyter, 2012).

3. See Mike Fabarez, *10 Mistakes People Make about Heaven, Hell, and the Afterlife* (Eugene, OR: Harvest House, 2018), especially chapter 5 ("Heaven Is Filled with Tract Homes and Government-Issued Uniforms," 81–98).

4. David H. Wenkel, "The Gnashing of Teeth of Jesus's Opponents," *Bibliotheca Sacra* 175 (2018): 83–95.

On the Sign Gifts of the Holy Spirit

1. The designation of certain gifts as "sign gifts" comes from 1 Corinthians 14:20–22, where the gifts of tongues and prophecy are described as signs for unbelievers and believers respectively (cf. 1 Cor. 1:22).

On Human Sexuality

1. Mary Eberstadt, *How the West Really Lost God, A New Theory of Secularization* (West Conshohocken, PA: Templeton Press, 2013), 161.

2. R. Albert Mohler Jr., *We Cannot Be Silent* (Nashville, TN: Nelson Books, 2015); quote from Mary Eberstadt, *Adam and Eve after the Pill: Paradoxes of the Sexual Revolution* (San Francisco: Ignatius Press, 2012), 12.

3. On the overall benefits of marriage and monogamy, especially for women and children, see Eberstadt, *How the West Really Lost God*, 24–31. See too, Eberstadt, *Adam and Eve after the Pill*.

4. See for example, D. Paul Sullins, "Invisible Victims: Delayed Onset Depression among Adults with Same-Sex Parents," *Depression Research and Treatment*, vol. 2016, Article ID 24103928, https://www.hindawi.com/journals/drt/2016/2410392/.

5. Peter L. Berger, *The Sacred Canopy: Elements of a Sociological Theory of Religion* (New York: Doubleday & Co., 1967).

6. Charles Taylor, *The Ethics of Authenticity*, (Cambridge, MA, and London, England: Harvard University Press, 1991).

7. Ibid., 29.

8. Multiple Faculty Contributors, "Genesis," in *The Moody Bible Commentary*, ed. Michael A. Rydelnik and Michael G. Vanlaningham (Chicago: Moody, 2014), 39.

9. 1967 US Supreme Court decision, *Loving v. Virginia*, available at Legal Information Institute, Cornell Law School, https://www.law.cornell.edu/supremecourt/text/388/1. Chief Justice Warren delivered the opinion of the

Court writing: "There is patently no legitimate overriding purpose independent of invidious racial discrimination which justifies this classification. The fact that Virginia prohibits only interracial marriages involving white persons demonstrates that the racial classifications must stand on their own justification, as measures designed to maintain White Supremacy. . . . The freedom to marry has long been recognized as one of the vital personal rights essential to the orderly pursuit of happiness by free men. . . . To deny this fundamental freedom on so unsupportable a basis as the racial classifications embodied in these statutes, classifications so directly subversive of the principle of equality at the heart of the Fourteenth Amendment, is surely to deprive all the State's citizens of liberty without due process of law."

10. *Supreme Court of the United States Syllabus Obergefell et al. versus Hodges, Director*, Ohio Department of Health, et al., October Term, 2014, decided June 26, 2015.
11. Lyle Denniston, "Constitutional Milestone on Transgender Rights," *Constitutional Daily* of the National Constitutional Center (4/16/2018), https://constitutioncenter.org/blog/constitutional-milestone-on-transgender-rights.
12. Alice Jones, "Redefining Gender," *National Geographic Magazine* (January 2017), https://www.nationalgeographic.com/magazine/2017/01/explore-gender-glossary-terminology/. For a recent mapping of sex, sexual orientation, gender, and gender identity, see the tutorials offered by Planned Parenthood, "Sexual Orientation and Gender," https://www.planned parenthood.org/learn/sexual-orientation-gender.
13. Charles Taylor, *A Secular Age* (Cambridge, MA: The Belknap Press of Harvard University Press, 2007).

Moving Forward with Steadfast, Humble Conviction

1. Charles C. Ryrie, *Basic Theology* (Chicago: Moody, 1999), 9.
2. My definition of *inspiration* is that God superintended or "buoyed along" (2 Peter 1:21) the human authors and used their own individual personalities in the production of Scripture, but that the end product in the original manuscripts penned by those authors (or their amanuenses) was His inerrant revelation to man. This differs from a mechanical dictation theory, which suggests that the personalities of the authors were somehow suspended, or that they were not active participants in the process that led to the production of Scripture. That inspiration, as noted in the chapter on authority, extends to the very words of Scripture as "God-breathed" (as God "spoke" them, guaranteeing their truthfulness in all they assert).
3. Ligonier Ministries, "The State of Theology," thestateoftheology.com; Kevin P. Emmert, "New Poll Finds Evangelicals' Favorite Heresies," *Christianity Today*, October 28, 2014, https://www.christianitytoday.com/ct/2014/october-web-only/new-poll-finds-evangelicals-favorite-heresies.html.
4. Indeed, the key distinction between Israel and the church, addressed partially in Brian Tucker's chapter pertaining to the MBI statement of ecclesiology, could be expanded into a much fuller treatment.
5. The reality of the level of biblical ignorance in the world today may require that we articulate once more, with clarity, what the Scriptures reveal as the gospel that Jesus intended the world to proclaim!

6. For the reader not familiar with the Reformation *solae*, they are embodied in the following Latin phrases: *sola Scriptura* ("Scripture alone") affirms the source of authority by which Protestants guide behavior and adjudicate truth. For Reformed Christians, Scripture must govern over church traditions and interpretations that are themselves held to be subject to Scripture. Church traditions, creeds, and teachings must be in unity with the teachings of Scripture. *Sola fide* ("by faith alone") affirms that justification is not accomplished through the merging of our works with our faith, nor do our works or anything external to us infuse us with grace. *Sola gratia* ("by grace alone") affirms that our salvation is totally an act of the grace of God extended to us; not generated in response to human action. *Solus Christus* or *Solo Christo* ("Christ alone" or "by Christ alone") identifies Christ as God's redeeming agent, the One through whom our salvation is wrought. Finally, *soli Deo gloria* ("glory to God alone") instructs that the purpose of God in saving us is for His glory and the honor for saving those who believe belongs to God and God only (and does not include veneration in the sense of lesser glory to other saints). In most of the earliest articulations of the *solae*, three were typically specified: the formal principle, which is Scripture over tradition; then faith over works; and finally grace over merit. Each expression was intended to represent an important distinction compared with heresies claimed in popular practice or in Catholic Church teachings.

INNOVATOR, EVANGELIST, WORLD-CHANGER

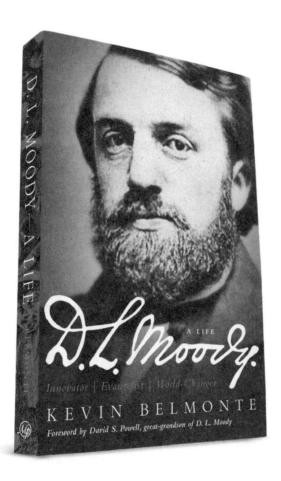

THE VISION AND WORLDWIDE IMPACT OF MOODY BIBLE INSTITUTE

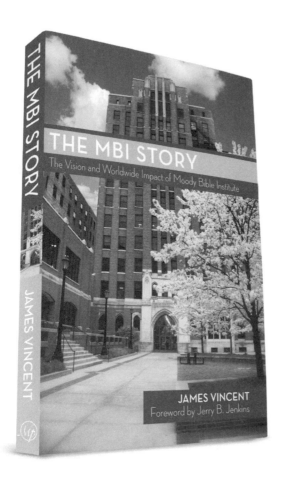

MOODY Publishers

From the Word to Life

The Moody Bible Institute celebrated 125 years of ministry in 2011. The "official" history of MBI was updated and released in time for Founder's Week in February 2011. This volume is the most comprehensive, up-to-date review of the history, ministry, and impact of the Moody Bible Institute of Chicago.

978-0-8024-5101-9 | also available as an eBook